Cambridge English

Objective
Proficiency

Workbook
with answers

T0343019

Peter Sunderland **Erica Whettem** **Second Edition**

Shaftesbury Road, Cambridge CB2 8EA, United Kingdom

One Liberty Plaza, 20th Floor, New York, NY 10006, USA

477 Williamstown Road, Port Melbourne, VIC 3207, Australia

314–321, 3rd Floor, Plot 3, Splendor Forum, Jasola District Centre, New Delhi – 110025, India

103 Penang Road, #05-06/07, Visioncrest Commercial, Singapore 238467

Cambridge University Press & Assessment is a department of the University of Cambridge.

We share the University's mission to contribute to society through the pursuit of education, learning and research at the highest international levels of excellence.

www.cambridge.org
Information on this title: www.cambridge.org/9781107619203

© Cambridge University Press & Assessment 2013

First published 2002
Second edition published 2013

40 39 38 37 36 35 34 33 32 31 30 29 28 27

Printed in Great Britain by Ashford Colour Press Ltd.

A catalogue record for this publication is available from the British Library

ISBN 978-1-107-61920-3 Workbook with answers with Audio CD
ISBN 978-1-107-62156-5 Workbook without answers with Audio CD
ISBN 978-1-107-64637-7 Student's Book with answers with Downloadable Software
ISBN 978-1-107-61116-0 Student's Book without answers with Downloadable Software
ISBN 978-1-107-67634-3 Class Audio CDs (2)
ISBN 978-1-107-67056-3 Teacher's Book
ISBN 978-1-107-63368-1 Student's Book Pack (Student's Book with answers with
Downloadable Software and Class Audio CDs (2)

Contents

Reading

1 You are going to read an article with the headline opposite. Think about the headline and choose the relationship (a–d) which you think the article is most likely to be about.

Sorry, honey, I shrunk your job prospects

a client–supplier
b boss–employee
c husband–wife
d parent–child

Quickly read the article to see if you were right.

2 Read the article and decide which paragraph (A–K) each of these cartoons refers to. Underline the sentence(s) or phrase(s) in the text that justify your answer.

1

2

3

4

5

6

3 Which of these *do's* and *don'ts* are mentioned in the article?
   Tick the boxes which apply and circle the sentence(s) or phrase(s) in the text that justify your answer.

a Do not overdo jewellery. ☐
b Attend lots of events. ☐
c Do not over-indulge in food or drink. ☐
d Exercise control when it comes to dancing. ☐
e Be discrete at all times. ☐
f Dress comfortably for all occasions. ☐
g Do not discuss topics of a religious nature. ☐

h Do not break into business discussions. ☐
i Do not refer to your spouse's business expertise. ☐
j Try to have a good time at corporate events. ☐
k Find out something about the host company before the event. ☐
l Give the impression of wanting to know more about the host company. ☐

A Charles Sacarello is talking about an ambitious executive who had almost reached the top of the corporate ladder. There was only one problem that threatened to block his career path – his wife. Bored and lonely sitting at home while her husband was out at work all day, she metamorphosed into a bulldozer at corporate events. She dominated conversations, ploughed her way through trays of canapés and never said 'no' to another glass of champagne.

B Socially inept spouses are Sacarello's bread and butter. The Gibraltar-born image consultant whose firm, Charles & Associates, has become popular in New York, teaches executives' wives – and husbands – how to behave at corporate functions. Spouses hire him for coaching on everything from table manners and how much jewellery to wear ('Don't look like a Christmas tree') to finding the right conversation filler. 'There are bright young men who have made it up the career ladder and their wives don't reflect the position they are trying to occupy,' he says.

C Sacarello's school for executive spouses has proved so popular that he now aims to build up a client base in the UK.

D In New York, Sacarello's clients are upwardly mobile and do a lot of work-related socialising. They are from modest economic backgrounds and range in age from early 20s to late 40s. The fee for an initial consultation is $500; some clients will spend as much as $10,000. They meet Sacarello, 45, and his partner, David Steinberg, 42, in a restaurant. 'We want to see them walk into a room,' Sacarello says. 'Do they skirt off into a corner? Or do they run up and say "hello" because they're nervous?'

E Some problems – mostly requiring restraint at the buffet table or on the dance floor – are easily solved. Others are more serious. Occasionally, Sacarello has to refer clients to a psychologist or a priest. Many of them are married to high-profile figures from the business and entertainment worlds, so discretion is key. In company files they are referred to by code names.

F 'There are people who have made money but it hasn't bought them polish or class,' Steinberg says. 'We want to boost their self-esteem so they feel comfortable walking into any situation.' Some of his tips are: avoid conversations about sex or religion, do not interrupt if people are talking about business, and never say how wonderful your spouse is in the corporate world.

G Steinberg encourages his clients to enjoy corporate events. 'Know a little bit about the company and show some interest,' he says. 'Our goal is that when two people walk into a room, nobody knows which one is the high-flier.'

H Husbands of high-flying female executives are Sacarello's newest clients. Bill Higgins, 55, a former FBI agent and retired naval captain, found the role of corporate spouse difficult at first. After his retirement in 1997 he started to accompany his wife Barbara Corcoran, 50, who manages Manhattan's largest privately owned real estate company, on business trips. 'I felt uncomfortable because I was the spouse and there were all these guys there who were younger and more successful than me,' he says. Spouses wore different coloured name badges, and Higgins would often be the only man at a table of 40 women, while his wife sat at another table with their husbands.

I Higgins is now so comfortable in his role that he carries a business card labelled 'spouse'. He has formed a men's group to advise other corporate spouses and has set up a website. Corcoran boasts that her husband is an asset at corporate events. 'He comes feeling accomplished and therefore he's willing to dance in my shadow,' she says.

J Her first husband was not so obliging: 'He was younger than me and not accomplished. He needed to prove his worth wherever we went. The most awkward moments were when people called him Mr Corcoran.'

K It is the Higgins–Corcoran brand of teamwork that impresses Sacarello. 'One of the main decisions in life is choosing your partner,' he says. 'If you've goofed on that one, how competent are you?'

4 Find a word or phrase in the article with these meanings (the paragraph letter is given in brackets).

a stand in the way of (A)
b skills training (B)
c not particularly wealthy (D)
d price charged (D)
e in the public eye (E)
f increase (F)
g successful achiever (G)
h a useful and valuable resource (I)
i willing to help or please (J)

Grammar

5 Complete the text with an appropriate form of the verbs in brackets. There may be more than one possible answer.

A new experience

I **(1)** .... (find) myself in some bizarre situations recently, but none so unusual as a few weeks ago, when I was lying on a black plastic mattress, covered from head to toe in oil, with a man walking all over me.

Incense **(2)** .... (burn) on a low table, the only sounds that of the sea and of crows ducking out of the way of an eagle. In some parts of the world this might **(3)** .... (be) part of some full-moon ritual, and I would **(4)** .... (be) concerned about my safety. But this **(5)** .... (be) the middle of another hot and slightly steamy day in southern India, and whatever **(6)** .... (happen) to me **(7)** .... (be done) in the name of health. I **(8)** .... (experience) my first Ayurveda rejuvenation massage.

Vocabulary

6 Complete the sentences using the verbs in the box, which all mean *change* in some way. You may need to change the form of the verb. Use your dictionary to help you. There may be more than one answer.

adapt	alter	amend	convert
develop	evolve	fluctuate	
metamorphose	modify	mutate	
revise	transform		

a The good thing about children is that they .... easily to new environments.

b I took the coat back to the shop to have it ....

c In line 20, 'men' should be .... to 'people'.

d The design proposals were unpopular and only accepted in a .... form.

e These bacteria have .... into forms that are resistant to certain drugs.

f The reorganisation will totally .... the British entertainment industry.

g The awkward boy I knew had .... into a tall, handsome man.

h They live in a .... windmill.

i How do we know that humans .... from apes?

j Vegetable prices .... according to the season.

k The bank manager forced them to .... their sales forecasts three times.

l What started out as a short story eventually .... into a full-scale novel.

7 Complete these sentences, which all include expressions with *change*, using the picture clues below and your dictionary to help you. Which of the sentences have no corresponding illustration?

EXAMPLE: She'd been with the same company such a long time, she felt she needed a change of *scene*.

a She'd always been against the proposed supermarket, but she soon changed her .... when she realised what they would pay for her land.

b That Italian restaurant is nowhere near as good since it changed ....

c He's so untidy! If he wants to live here, he's going to have to change his ....

d When I first met him, I didn't like him, but now I've changed my ....

e I wouldn't change .... with him for the world!

f She took a change of .... in her suitcase as they were staying overnight.

g Let's change the .... or we'll end up arguing again.

8 Replace the verbs in italics in sentences a–m with an appropriate two- or three-part phrasal verb made by combining the verbs and prepositions in the table below. You may need to change the form of the verb and the word order. Use your dictionary to help you.

EXAMPLE: He paused for a moment to listen and then continued eating.

*He paused for a moment to listen and then **carried on** eating.*

a She came out of the shop to find thieves had *stolen* her bicycle.

b The chaos in the house was starting to *depress* him.

c I feel like I'm getting nowhere with my online campaign. I keep *encountering* a wall of hostility.

d Boy, will I be glad to *finish* these exams!

e I typed in 'swimming technique' on a search engine and literally thousands of websites *appeared*.

f He has to *submit* the application form by Friday.

g News of someone's pregnancy soon *spreads*.

h You'll find my enthusiasm more than *offsets* my lack of experience.

i How successful were they in *conveying* the message, do you think?

j The hospital is *conducting* tests to find out what is wrong with her.

k Could you *despatch* the parcel this morning, please?

l The football manager tried an elaborate new tactic but it didn't *work*.

m Look, I really can't come, sorry; something important has *arisen*.

~~carry~~	across	against
carry	around	for
come	down	with
come	in	with
come	off	
come	off	
get	off	
get	~~on~~	
get	out	
get	over	
get	up	
get	up	
make	up	
make	up	

9 Look at the idioms in bold, and the three possible sentences containing them. Put a tick (✓) if the sentence is correct and a cross (✗) if it's wrong.

a Sorry, I've **lost track of** what we're supposed to be doing. ☐
Sorry, I've **lost track of** you since we were at school together. ☐
Sorry, I've **lost track of** that new coat you gave me. ☐

b **It never crossed my mind** that I'd agreed to sign the document. ☐
It never crossed my mind to ask for a refund. ☐
It never crossed my mind that he would actually carry out his threat! ☐

c **Look on the bright side** – you could be back home bored out of your wits! ☐
Look on the bright side – you might still be able to get hold of tickets online. ☐
Look on the bright side – you would be very unhappy if this happened to you! ☐

d Being a ski rep in Austria **is a far cry from** my old job in the factory back home! ☐
The calling sound the bird makes **is a far cry from** trying to contact its mate. ☐
What we're witnessing here **is a far cry from** a desperate man who's lost his way. ☐

e **I'll keep you posted** if you would be so kind. ☐
I'll keep you posted if what you're claiming is true. ☐
I'll keep you posted if there are any further developments. ☐

f Look, just to **set the record straight** – I'm afraid we can't accept your application. ☐
Davidson needs just one more win to **set the record straight**. ☐
The manager assumed that Agnes and Derek were married, but she soon **set the record straight**. ☐

2 Expectation

Listening

1 🔊02 You will hear five different people (1–5) talking about the first time they flew abroad by themselves, and the expectations they had. For questions 1–5, choose from the list A–F what each speaker said. There is one statement that you will not need.

A I knew from experience what to expect.
B My expectations were confirmed.
C It was a life-changing event for me.
D I appreciated the trip more as I was alone.
E It was very different from what I'd imagined.
F I found it quite similar to being at home.

Speaker 1	**1**	
Speaker 2	**2**	
Speaker 3	**3**	
Speaker 4	**4**	
Speaker 5	**5**	

2 🔊02 Listen again and fill each gap with one word from the recording to complete these expressions.

a (Speaker 1) I didn't .... what to expect

b (Speaker 1) from that .... on

c (Speaker 1) well and truly ....

d (Speaker 2) nothing .... for me

e (Speaker 2) .... nature to me

f (Speaker 2) have no .... but to

g (Speaker 2) .... to the challenge

h (Speaker 2) sink or ....

i (Speaker 3) it was a great ....

j (Speaker 3) .... up the atmosphere

k (Speaker 4) an .... mind

l (Speaker 4) .... to the test

m (Speaker 5) a once in a .... opportunity

3 Re-use some of the expressions in similar situations:

a
My first day as a travel agent was tough, as the office was busy with customers. The things I'd learnt in training were really .... On the whole, I think I .... well, but there was one query I simply couldn't answer, and I had .... call my boss for help.

b
On a recent trip to Spain, I went to watch Barcelona play Real Madrid. I'd never been to such a huge stadium before, and I arrived early so as to .... In my country the standard of football is much lower, so for me .... to see the incredible skill of the players. After such a fantastic match, I was .... on Spanish football.

c
My first ever interview was for a place at university, and not surprisingly .... , so it was all rather new and intimidating for me. A lot was at stake, so it was a real .... situation. But the interviewer told a joke to put me at my ease, and .... I was much happier.

Grammar

4 Complete these extracts with an appropriate form of the verbs in the box. You may also need to use *will/shall* on their own. There may be more than one correct answer.

| be (× 3) | be on the verge of | give | leave | open |
| pack (× 2) | visit | | | |

Thanks very much for the invite to dinner this evening – I
(1) .... able to make it though. I'm off to
Mexico in the morning (my plane (2) ....
at 5 am!) and I (3) .... hard-pushed to get
ready in time. It looks like I (4) .... into
the small hours. My company (5) ....
an office there next month and apparently some problem's
come up with the lease they (6) ....
signing. Anyhow, I'm really sorry about this evening but
(7) .... we do something together at
the weekend? I (8) .... my grandmother
at some point during the day on Sunday, but otherwise I
(9) .... free till the end of next week.
That (10) .... me something to look
forward to while I (11) .... suitcases
tonight! Let me know how you're fixed.

| acquire | also consider | be (× 2) | develop |
| also | expect | | |

JOBS IN SCIENCE

Earth Observation Applications Scientist

Leading a specialist team, you (12) ....
a generic synthetic aperture radar (SAR) image-focusing
processor, with the aim of producing a cost-effective high
performance space radar within two years. Ideally you
(13) .... a minimum of five years'
experience in signal-processing applications plus signal-
simulation experience, though candidates with less experience
but with a highly relevant academic background
(14) ....

Excellent computing skills (15) ....
necessary and you (16) .... to have
a good understanding of advanced engineering mathematics.
Proven analytical and presentation skills
(17) .... essential to your success,
as (18) .... your effective use of IT
systems.

| be likely | break | expect | have |
| move | remain | | |

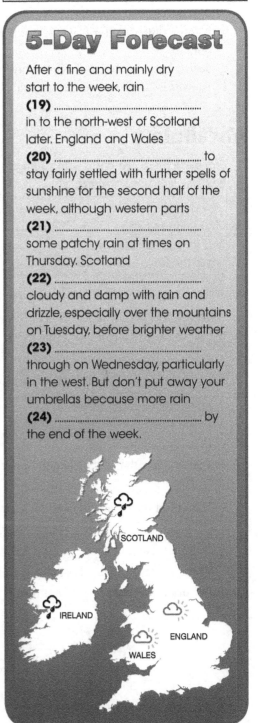

5-Day Forecast

After a fine and mainly dry
start to the week, rain
(19) ....
in to the north-west of Scotland
later. England and Wales
(20) .... to
stay fairly settled with further spells of
sunshine for the second half of the
week, although western parts
(21) ....
some patchy rain at times on
Thursday. Scotland
(22) ....
cloudy and damp with rain and
drizzle, especially over the mountains
on Tuesday, before brighter weather
(23) ....
through on Wednesday, particularly
in the west. But don't put away your
umbrellas because more rain
(24) .... by
the end of the week.

SCOTLAND

IRELAND

ENGLAND

WALES

5 Put the missing punctuation into these sentences from the *Cambridge Learner Corpus*, written by Profiency candidates. There is one mistake in each sentence.

a In a few years time, there is the risk of having to …

b What about going to your aunts to spend Christmas?

c As a young woman she started educating young black children.

d She was called to Washington D.C. where she joined the Advisory Board.

e Her mother, who was in the kitchen heard that she wanted to …

f A longer life therefore, means not only more opportunities but also …

g Seeing her you wouldn't believe how nice she is.

h I saw this could, at least temporarily improve our situation.

Vocabulary

6 Complete these sentences using a prepositional phrase from the box. Use a dictionary to help you.

at odds with	beyond all expectation
by no means	in all honesty
on its own merits	out of my control
over the top	within reason

a It's .... certain that the job will go to an external candidate.

b You can invite anyone you like to my birthday party, ...

c I can assure you that each of your proposals will be judged ....

d John's angry reaction to my letter was completely ....

e Clare's claim that she locked the door behind her is .... what she said earlier.

f You could try to get a refund on your ticket, but .... I don't think there's much point.

g Ivan's English improved .... when he stayed with a host family in Manchester.

h I've done all I can for you, but ultimately the matter is ....

7 Using an appropriate word from the box with *have no*, replace the words in italics so that each sentence has the **opposite** meaning. You will also need to change the form of some verbs and you may need to add a preposition or *but*. Use your dictionary to help you.

appeal	chance	desire
doubt	option	problem
qualms	~~recollection~~	

EXAMPLE: Apparently, he *remembered* our meeting last March. *Apparently, he **had no recollection of** our meeting last March.*

a Having known him for years, she *didn't believe* that he was lying.

....

b They *found it difficult* to follow the instructions that they had been given.

....

c Eng *really wanted* to go back to her home country before she died.

....

d Sara *was unhappy* about lying to the police.

....

e I *will be able to* finish this essay before the weekend.

....

f Having run out of money, Bogdan *chose* to work.

....

g Going to the theatre *was a treat* after everything she had been through.

....

Use of English

8 Read the text below. Use the word given in capitals at the end of some of the lines to form a word that fits in the gap in the same line. There is an example at the beginning (0).

More people fly today than ever before, yet many – experienced air (0) ....*travellers*....	TRAVEL
as well as novices – suffer anguish and (1) .... at the mere thought	APPREHEND
of flying. As many as one in seven people are thought to experience anxiety	
when flying, with women (2) .... men two to one in these feelings	NUMBER
of (3)	QUIET
A certain amount of concern is (4) .... The sheer size of modern	UNDERSTAND
jet aircraft, which appear awkward and (5) .... on the ground, makes	WIELD
one wonder how they will manage to get into the air – and stay there. However,	
most of these fears are (6) .... and are perhaps based on the knowledge	LOGIC
that once in the aircraft, we, as passengers, are (7) .... to control our	POWER
fate, which depends solely on the (8) .... of the crew. There is little	EXPERT
comfort for us in the numerous statistical compilations which show	
that modern air transport is many times safer than transport by	
car or rail.	

9 Read the text below and think of the word which best fits each gap. Use only one word in each gap. There is an example at the beginning (0).

By the **(0)** .....*time*..... we landed in Oslo, it was already pitch dark. Rather than the wintry wonderland I had hoped **(1)** ...., rain was lashing down under the orange airport lights. It was bitterly cold. The airport bus deposited me, tired, hungry and disorientated, in the city centre. After several wrong turns, and **(2)** .... nearly dislocated my shoulders with the weight of my backpack, I finally stumbled into the reception of my chosen, but unbooked, hotel. **(3)** .... my horror, I discovered that every hotel in the centre was fully booked **(4)** .... to a pop concert. The receptionist redirected me to the tramline and some possible bed and breakfast places way **(5)** .... in the suburbs. Two hours **(6)** .... I stood in the rain, peering around in vain, cursing the pop singer to the Oslo night sky. Eventually, I hauled my weary limbs along a dark and muddy path, at the end of **(7)** .... I found the shining lights of a small hotel. 'Vacancies' **(8)** .... a sign on the door.

Reading

1 You are going to read an article about human behaviour. For questions 1–10, choose from the sections (A–D). The sections may be chosen more than once.

Which section mentions ...

a strong reaction to news of the writer's research?	1 ☐
one animal showing jealousy?	2 ☐
an animal thinking of the consequences of their actions?	3 ☐
any unfairness provoking a strong and selfish reaction?	4 ☐
the animal behaviour shown not going as far as equivalent human behaviour?	5 ☐
a sense of injustice from people having to cope with adverse conditions?	6 ☐
an explanation for the irrational sense of unfairness that humans or animals may show?	7 ☐
an animal's feeling of injustice leading to irrational behaviour?	8 ☐
unfairness among humans being perceived by those who are less well off?	9 ☐
examples of both humans and animals behaving with fairness?	10 ☐

It's not fair!

Do animals share our sense of unfairness over displays of greed?

A How often have you seen rich people take to the streets, shouting that they're earning too much? Protesters are typically blue-collar workers yelling that the minimum wage has to go up, or that their jobs shouldn't go overseas. Concern about fairness is always asymmetrical, stronger in the poor than the rich. And the underlying emotions aren't as lofty as the ideal itself. Children become thoroughly indignant at the slightest discrepancy in, say, the size of their slice of pizza compared to their sibling's. Their shouts of 'That's not fair!' never transcend their own desires. We're all for fair play so long as it helps us. There's an old story about this, in which the owner of a vineyard rounds up labourers at different times of day. Early in the morning he went out to find labourers, offering each 1 denarius. But he offered the same to those hired later in the day. The workers hired first thing in the morning expected to get more since they had worked through the heat of the day, yet the owner didn't feel he owed them any more than he'd originally promised.

B That this sense of unfairness may turn out to be quite ancient in evolutionary terms as well became clear when graduate student Sarah Brosnan and I discovered it in monkeys. When testing pairs of capuchin monkeys, we noticed how much they disliked seeing their partner get a better deal. We would offer a pebble to one of the pair and then hold out a hand so that the monkey could give it back in exchange for a cucumber slice. Alternating between them, both monkeys would happily barter 25 times in a row. The atmosphere turned sour, however, as soon as we introduced inequality. One monkey would still receive cucumber, while its partner now enjoyed grapes, a favourite food with monkeys. While that monkey had no problem, the one still working for cucumber would lose interest. Worse, seeing its partner with juicy grapes, this monkey would get agitated, hurl the pebbles out of the test chamber, sometimes even those measly cucumber slices. A food normally devoured with gusto had become distasteful.

C There is a similarity here with the way we reject an unfair share of money. Where do such reactions come from? They probably evolved in the service of cooperation. Caring about what others get may seem petty and irrational, but in the long run it keeps one from being taken advantage of. Had we merely mentioned emotions, such as resentment or envy, our findings might have gone unnoticed. Now we drew the interest of philosophers, anthropologists and economists, who almost choked on the monkey comparison. As it happened, our study came out at the very time that there was a public outcry about the multimillion dollar pay packages that are occasionally given out on Wall Street and elsewhere. Commentators couldn't resist contrasting human society with our monkeys, suggesting that we could learn a thing or two from them.

D Our monkeys have not reached the point at which their sense of fairness stretches beyond egocentric interests – for example, the one who gets the grape never levels the outcome by giving it to the other – but in cooperative human societies, such as those in which men hunt large game, anthropologists have found great sensitivity to equal distribution. Sometimes, successful hunters aren't even allowed to carve up their own kill to prevent them from favouring their family. These cultures are keenly aware of the risk that inequity poses to the social fabric of their society. Apes, as opposed to monkeys, may have an inkling of this connection. High-ranking male chimpanzees, for example, sometimes break up fights over food without taking any for themselves. During tests, a female received large amounts of milk and raisins, but noticed her friends watching her from a short distance. After a while, she refused all rewards. Looking at the experimenter, she kept gesturing to the others, until they were given a share of the goodies. She was doing the smart thing. Apes think ahead, and if she had eaten her fill right in front of the rest, there might have been repercussions when she rejoined them later in the day.

Grammar

2 Identify the incorrect verb form in these sentences, then rewrite each sentence correctly starting with the word in brackets.

EXAMPLE: The tourist party might actually have seen a gorilla in the flesh if the weather were a little more favourable.
(Had …)

were → had been
Had the weather **been** a little more favourable, the tourist party might actually have seen a gorilla in the flesh.

a There should be no problem in arranging that loan for you unless you will fail to meet our terms and conditions. (Provided …)

b If you would happen to notice anything strange, kindly make a note of it for me.
(Should …)

c Were jetlag a figment of the imagination, air travellers had no problems on arrival at their destination.
(If …)

d As the sun should cause permanent damage to your eyes, you shouldn't look directly at it.
(Given that …)

e This planet would be heading for destruction, unless we pay more attention to environmental issues.
(If …)

f Provided you stay calm, we would be able to assess the situation quickly.
(If …)

g If we hadn't had luck on our side, we hadn't ever survived the storm and returned safe and sound.
(Without …)

h If there is a red sky at night, it is fine the next day. (As long as …)

i If you spend long periods of time above 5500 metres, you must experience the ill effects of altitude.
(Provided … not)

j You wouldn't have this wonderful evidence to support your theory now, if you didn't persevere with your research. (But for …)

k Unless you took time to acclimatise when you arrive in a hot country, you will be asking for trouble.
(As long as …)

l I'll agree to come to the party as long as you haven't worn those ridiculous trousers.
(On condition that …)

Vocabulary

3 The words in capitals after these sentences are all anagrams of nouns meaning *behaviour*. Use the context and your dictionary to help you solve them and fill the gaps. The first and last letters are given.

EXAMPLE: It's considered good **m**anne**r**s in some societies to leave a little food on your plate. RENMANS

a Over the years we've got used to his funny little **w**.................**s**. YAWS

b His **a**.................**s** since that morning have been quite eccentric and unpredictable. NOCTIAS

c The president surprised everyone with his unusual **c**.................**t** at the memorial service. TUNCCOD

d She walked at the head of the procession, her **b**.................**g** proud and distinguished. GIRABEN

e When their favourite player was sent off, the **r**.................**n** of the crowd was very hostile. TEANIORC

f There was nothing in his **d**.................**r** that suggested he was anxious. REUMANDEO

g His eating **h**.................**s** are rather extraordinary. STIHBA

4 Correct any words in these sentences which are used or spelled incorrectly.

a The Santa Ana wind can have a dramatic affect on people in Los Angeles.

b In some extreme weather conditions, people have been known to loose control.

c Certain weather patterns are associated with a raise in crime rates.

d Predicting the weather accurately takes more than practise.

e My grandfather believes in weather lore like his ansestors before him.

f The day the weather forecasters took industrious action was an interesting day for the nation.

g Some people believe animal behaviour could offer a viable alternate means of earthquake detection.

h Beside being struck twice by lightning, she has also had some experiences of hurricanes.

5 Use words from the box to find collocations with the words in bold and complete the sentences. Use your dictionary to help you.

feeling	intuition	~~misgivings~~	omen
sense	sight	sign	suspicion

EXAMPLE: Many teachers have expressed **serious** *misgivings* about the new exams.

a Those black clouds are a **sure** .... of rain.

b I once met a man with **second** .... who told me I was going to lose my job – and I did.

c I had a **funny** .... that you'd show up!

d I've got a **sneaking** .... that we're going the wrong way.

e We hoped that the delay at the airport was not a **bad** .... for our holiday.

f She seemed to have a **sixth** .... when it came to knowing what her twin was thinking.

g When a woman anticipates something, it is sometimes put down to **female** ....

6 The words in the box are all nouns that express strong emotions. Put each one in the correct sentence below to complete the collocations in bold.

disgust	fears	frustration
guilt	rage	tedium

a Margaret was **haunted by** .... at the terrible things she'd done.

b To **relieve the** .... of the journey, John looked out of the window and counted passing trucks.

c When I told him what had happened, the manager **exploded with** ....

d 'Look, it's annoying, but it's not my fault! Don't **vent your** .... on me!

e I hope I have succeeded in **allaying your** .... about the future of the company.

f I could scarcely **conceal my** .... at his table manners.

Use of English

7 Read the text below and decide which answer (A, B, C or D) best fits each gap. There is an example at the beginning (0).

TIGERS AS PETS

They may be (0) ....A.... extinction in India, China and Siberia, but in the US, tigers have found a new lease of life – after a fashion. More than 12,000 are kept as pets – double the number thought to exist in the wild. The craze persists (1) .... concern among politicians and animal welfare groups. Various reputable organisations promote ownership of endangered species. Prices are not particularly (2) .... : $1,000 for a generic cub, $3,500 for a pair of Bengal tigers.

The private trade originated in zoos. Tiger cubs (3) .... so popular with the public that zoos started breeding more than they needed and sold the (4) .... to private breeders. The US Endangered Species Act of 1973 outlaws the taking of endangered animals from the wild, but does not (5) .... what happens to the offspring of animals captured before the law was (6) ....

Many owners believe they are saving an endangered species. But their cubs have no (7) .... among wild tigers. They are a mixture of, (8) .... , Sumatran, Siberian and Bengal tigers, which would not survive in the wild.

0 **A** facing	**B** reaching	**C** getting	**D** meeting
1 **A** in contrast to	**B** nevertheless	**C** in spite of	**D** whereas
2 **A** forbidding	**B** prohibitive	**C** impossible	**D** restraining
3 **A** occurred	**B** demonstrated	**C** established	**D** proved
4 **A** surplus	**B** balance	**C** residue	**D** leftovers
5 **A** rule	**B** conduct	**C** systematise	**D** regulate
6 **A** sentenced	**B** issued	**C** passed	**D** stated
7 **A** equivalent	**B** similarity	**C** substitute	**D** correspondent
8 **A** imagine	**B** say	**C** suppose	**D** take

4 Sweet rituals

Listening

1 **[03]** You will hear three different extracts. For questions 1–6, choose the answer (A, B or C) which fits best according to what you hear. There are two questions for each extract.

Extract One

You hear a man talking about a harvest festival in China.

1 What is important to the man when eating a watermelon?
   A its outward appearance
   B its weight
   C its flesh

2 What impressed the man most about the festival?
   A the trade opportunities
   B the educational dimension
   C the cultural side

Extract Two

You hear part of an interview in which a journalist is talking about cookery books.

3 What is the journalist's main criticism of large cookbooks?
   A The amount of information is slight.
   B The recipes often prove to be unreliable.
   C The quality of the photography is patchy.

4 What is unique about William Verrall's book, according to the journalist?
   A the ingredients it uses
   B its focus on the negative
   C the strength of its humour

Extract Three

You hear a woman talking about her recent experience at a top-class restaurant.

5 What did the she admire for its presentation?
   A the spicy steak
   B the barbecued fish
   C the vegetarian option

6 What aspect of the restaurant was the woman somewhat disappointed with?
   A the décor
   B the furniture
   C the atmosphere

2 The recordings contain the phrasal verbs in 1–8 below. Match them to their meanings a–h.

1	engage with	*there are things for tourists to **engage with** too*
2	thumb through	*you've also **been thumbing through** some of the titles in a new series*
3	serve up	*the typical glossy publishing **we've been served up with** for the last couple of decades*
4	open up	*these books **open up** new vistas*
5	come up with	*but none **comes up with** observations like Verrall's*
6	hanker after	*They … seemed to **hanker after** my blackened cod*
7	do out in	*the room, which **was done out in** subtle shades of blue and cream*
8	live up to	*the food **lived up to** our expectations*

a skim read a lot of text
b be as good as
c decorate in a certain way
d show interest in
e create or reveal
f present to the public
g long for
h think of or suggest

3 Extract Three features adjectives describing flavour – *appetising*, and texture – *tender*. Which of the adjectives below describe flavour and which describe texture? Write *F* (flavour) or *T* (texture). Some adjectives can describe both. Use a dictionary to help you. The first one is done for you.

bland	F	grainy		mushy		sharp
creamy		insipid		overripe		stale
delectable		mild		palatable		tasteless
fibrous		moist		pulpy		watery

Grammar

4 Complete this extract from the introduction to a book by Indian cookery writer Madhur Jaffrey, using an appropriate form of the verbs in brackets. Be careful to use a passive, *would / used to* or a modal where necessary. There may be more than one correct answer.

I (0) ...... *have always loved* ...... (always love) to eat well. My mother once (1) .... (inform) me that my passion (2) .... (date back) to the hour of my birth when my grandmother (3) .... (write) the sacred syllable 'Om' on my tongue with a finger dipped in fresh honey. I (4) .... (apparently observe) smacking my lips rather loudly.

Starting from that time, food – good food – (5) .... (just appear) miraculously from somewhere at the back of our house in Delhi. It (6) .... (precede) by the most tantalising odours and the sounds of crockery and cutlery on the move. Soon we (7) .... (all sit) around the dinner table, engrossed in eating monsoon mushrooms cooked with coriander and turmeric, fish that my brothers (8) .... (just catch) in the Jamuna River and cubes of lamb smothered in a yoghurt sauce.

Indian food (9) .... (be) far more varied than the menus of Indian restaurants (10) .... (suggest). One of my fondest memories of school in Delhi (11) .... (be) of the lunches that we (12) .... (all bring) from our homes, ensconced in multi-tiered lunchboxes. My stainless steel lunchbox (13) .... (dangle) from the handle of my bicycle as I (14) .... (ride) at great speed to school every morning, my ribboned pigtails fluttering behind me. When the lunch bell finally (15) .... (set) us free, my friends and I (16) .... (assemble) under a shady tree if it (17) .... (be) summer or on a sunny verandah if it (18) .... (be) winter. My mouth (19) .... (begin) to water even before we (20) .... (open up) our lunchboxes. Eating (21) .... (always fill) us with a sense of adventure and discovery as we (22) .... (can) not always anticipate what the others (23) .... (bring).

Vocabulary

5 All the verbs in the box are used in collocations in the context of food. Choose one for each sentence below, changing the form of the verb where necessary.

> bolt   chew   devour   dine
> munch   polish off

a In awe, we watched as the snake .... the bird whole.

b The man gave his dog a bone to .... on.

c Mia was sitting there, ... happily on an apple from her lunch box.

d 'Don't .... your food or you'll get indigestion,' warned Sam's granny.

e In the restaurant by the lake, we .... like kings, as the food was so delicious and reasonably priced.

f The young man was so ravenous he ate a huge chicken dinner and then .... a large apple pie.

6 Complete these compound adjectives with a word that fits. There may be more than one correct answer. Use your dictionary to help you.

EXAMPLE: ice-*cold* water

a a thirst-.. drink

b a mouth-.. smell

c a fast-.. outlet

d free-.. eggs

e low-.. yoghurt

f fresh-.. bread

g stir-.. vegetables

h wafer-.. slices

i sun-.. tomatoes

j soft-.. chocolates

k full-.. wine

l home-.. food

Use of English

7 Read the text below and think of the word which best fits each gap. Use only one word in each gap. There is an example at the beginning (0).

Tasteless tomatoes

The average supermarket tomato is a depressing specimen: perfectly round, uniformly red, full of water, and almost (0) ...*without*... exception, utterly devoid (1) .... taste. In one consumer survey after (2) .... , these mass-produced fruits rate among the (3) .... disappointing contents of our shopping bags. Supermarkets care about four things: size, weight, sameness and colour; (4) .... taste. They consider flavour an irrelevance. But a properly grown, raw fruit, served (5) .... nature intended – and what I (6) .... by that is fresh off a vine and preferably still warm from the sun – is one of life's great pleasures. It should explode (7) .... impact with your mouth and be eatable only by slurping! It should be (8) .... fragile as to be impossible to handle without causing damage. Herein lies the problem for a commercial producer. To arrive on a supermarket shelf, a tomato must survive roughly a week of picking, packing and shipping. Unsurprising, then, that the supermarket version is not the real thing.

8 Complete the second sentence so that it has a similar meaning to the first sentence using the word given. Do not change the word given. You must use between three and eight words, including the word given.

EXAMPLE:

0 Having bad table manners is the most annoying thing!

nothing

There's ....*nothing more annoying than people*........ with bad table manners.

1 The Portuguese probably introduced chilli peppers to Asia.

thought

Chilli peppers ....

to Asia by the Portuguese.

2 People think he succeeded through hard work and determination.

put

People ....

hard work and determination.

3 Finnish people consume more coffee than any other Europeans.

consumption

Finland ....

country in Europe.

4 Everyone must have noticed the change in temperature.

failed

No one ....

the change in temperature.

5 The chef even revealed the secret ingredient in his winning recipe.

far

The chef went ....

the secret ingredient in his winning recipe.

6 The organisers went out of their way to help.

not

The organisers could ....

helpful.

Reading

You are going to read an article about a new phenomenon called ethical shopping. For questions 1–6, choose the answer (A, B, C or D) which you think fits best according to the text.

The problem with **ethical shopping**

Now I'm as environmentally concerned as the next man, probably more so, in fact, but a spate of new books urging us to live 'better, greener lifestyles' and to 'live within nature's limits' leaves me rather cold. Evidently, it's easy. Buy products that don't exploit other humans, animals or the environment. Don't shop at the multinational supermarkets, support small shops which sell environmentally friendly products, buy local produce when you need to, and, while you're about it, just make your own bread, butter, cheese, jam, keep a milking cow, a few pigs, goats, chickens, beehives, gardens and orchards. Well, what are you waiting for?

The book *A Slice of Organic Life* by Sheherazade Goldsmith contains plenty of useful advice, and she comes across as modest, sincere and well-informed. But of lobbying for political change, there is not a word. According to Goldsmith, you can save the planet from your own kitchen – if you have endless time and plenty of land. When I was reading it on the train, another passenger asked me if he could take a look. He flicked through it for a moment, and then summed up the problem in seven words: 'This is for people who don't work.'

The media's obsession with beauty, wealth and fame blights every issue it touches, but none more so than green issues. There is an inherent conflict between the aspirational lifestyle journalism that makes readers feel better about themselves and sells country-style kitchens to those who can afford them, and the central demand of environmentalism – that we should consume less. 'None of these changes represents a sacrifice,' Goldsmith tells us. 'Being more conscientious isn't about giving up things.' But it is if, like her, you own more than one home when others have none. Uncomfortable as this is for both the media and its advertisers, giving things up is an essential component of going green. A section on ethical shopping in Goldsmith's book advises us to buy organic, buy seasonal, buy local, buy sustainable, buy recycled. But it says nothing about buying less.

Green consumerism is becoming a pox on the planet. If it merely swapped the damaging goods we buy for less damaging ones, I would champion it. But two parallel markets are developing – one for unethical products and one for ethical products, and the expansion of the second does little to hinder the growth of the first. I am now drowning in a tide of ecojunk. Over the past six months, I have come to learn that organic cotton bags – filled with packets of ginseng tea and jojoba oil bath salts – are now the obligatory gift at every environmental event. I have several lifetimes' supply of ballpoint pens made with recycled paper and about half a dozen miniature solar chargers for gadgets that I do not possess.

Last week one leading newspaper told its readers not to abandon the fight to save the planet. 'There is still hope, and the middle classes, with their composters and eco-gadgets, will be leading the way.' It made some helpful suggestions, such as a 'hydrogen-powered model racing car', which, for £74.99, comes with a solar panel, an electrolyser and a fuel cell. One wonders what rare metals and energy-intensive processes were used to manufacture it. In the name of environmental consciousness, we have simply created new opportunities for surplus capital.

Green consumerism is becoming a pox on the planet

But there is another danger with ethical shopping. I have met houseowners who have bought solar panels and wind turbines before they have done the simple thing and insulated their lofts, partly because they love gadgets but partly, I suspect, because everyone can then see how conscientious and how rich they are. We are often told that buying such products encourages us to think more widely about environmental challenges, but it is just as likely to be depoliticising. Green consumerism is a substitute for collective action. No political challenge can be met by shopping.

Challenge the new green consumerism and you become a prig and a party pooper. Against the shiny new world of organic aspirations you are forced to raise boring restraints: carbon rationing, contraction and convergence, tougher building regulations, coach lanes on motorways. No newspaper will carry an article about that. But these measures, and the long hard political battle that is needed to bring them about, are unfortunately what is required. ■

1 By using the phrase 'Well, what are you waiting for?' (lines 11–12), the writer is emphasising
   A the impossibility of what is being proposed.
   B the urgency of the environmental problem.
   C how unclear it is as to what action is required.
   D how long it will take to change people's mindsets.

2 In the third paragraph, the writer disagrees with Sheherazade Goldsmith on
   A how people will react to being told how to run their lives.
   B how the media can best promote the concept of ethical shopping.
   C the need for the media to get involved in environmental matters.
   D the need for people to make sacrifices.

3 What is the writer saying in the fourth paragraph about the growth of ethical products?
   A It has a part to play in limiting waste.
   B It goes hand-in-hand with lack of quality.
   C It creates its own unnecessary demand.
   D It results in items that are ever more expensive.

4 What irony does the writer pick up on in the fifth paragraph?
   A The supposedly 'green' substance used to fuel the car is harmful.
   B The production of the car contributes to environmental damage.
   C The cost of the car puts it beyond the reach of those who would benefit from it.
   D The target market for the car is people who cause the most environmental problems.

5 What is the 'danger with ethical shopping' that the writer refers to in the sixth paragraph?
   A It may lead to unfair situations.
   B It could become a political tool.
   C It is becoming a signifier of social status.
   D It encourages us to save money in the wrong areas.

6 What is the writer's position on ethical shopping in the article as a whole?
   A It has become a plaything for the super rich.
   B There is very little in it which is new or relevant.
   C It has served its purpose and should now be replaced.
   D There is a better way of tackling environmental issues.

Grammar

2 Which of these nouns are countable, which are uncountable and which can be either? Use your dictionary to help you complete the table. The first one has been done for you.

Noun	Countable	Uncountable	Noun	Countable	Uncountable
advice	X	✓	machinery		
appliance			money		
business			parking		
cash			preference		
clothing			produce		
competition			product		
complaint			promotion		
equipment			publicity		
experience			right		
furniture			shopping		
information			success		

3 Use words from exercise 2 to complete these sentences. Where necessary add *a/an*, *the*, *some* or *any*. There may be more than one correct answer.

a You've bought a lovely house and it will look great once you get .... in.

b When my grandmother was a child, ... such as washing machines and dishwashers did not exist.

c We have received .... about our new service from a dissatisfied customer in Sweden.

d A huge percentage of new products coming to the market will fail; .... are surprisingly hard to achieve.

e Sorry I can't come, but I've been asked to take part in .... It's for my company's new skin care range.

f Apparently .... at the new store is free to drivers who spend over a certain sum there.

g If there is a choice of colours, do you have .... ?

h .... generated by the court case is hardly what the manufacturers would have wanted.

i When credit and debit cards are so widely accepted these days, I don't see the point in carrying ....

j Although he enjoys his work, he tries hard not to let .... interfere with pleasure.

k .... in the retail sector are likely to see their profits hit.

l By entering .... every week, she reckons on winning something at least four times a year!

m .... from overseas has prompted many manufacturing companies to slash their costs.

4 Which of the verb forms in italics in these sentences are correct? Sometimes the singular verb is correct, sometimes the plural verb is correct and sometimes both are correct. Delete the options which *don't* apply.

EXAMPLE: Athletics *is/are* on TV this afternoon.

a Belongings *is/are* sometimes a burden.
b Your clothes *is/are* very smart.
c The committee *votes/vote* on the issue tonight.
d The economy *is/are* in a state of decline.
e A new family *has/have* moved in next door.
f The goods *is/are* scheduled for delivery next week.
g The government *is/are* expected to announce new proposals.
h Management *has/have* offered staff a 3% pay rise.
i The news *is/are* on at 10 p.m.
j The police *is/are* investigating fraud allegations against him.
k Their premises *was/were* demolished last year.
l The public *is/are* not interested in the lives of second-rate popstars.
m Our swimming team *is/are* the best.
n The United States of America *has/have* been the world's principal economic power.

Vocabulary

5 Which of the topic areas below do the words in the box belong to? Complete the word spiders accordingly. Use your dictionary to help you. The first one has been done for you.

affluence	consumers	credit note	customers
defect	department store	designers	faulty goods
image	Internet	legal rights	lifestyle
mail order	malpractice	money back	possessions
retailers	returns	sales assistants	shopaholics
shoppers	status	supermarket	superstore

1

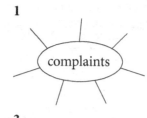
complaints

2

sales outlets

3
affluence

aspirations/ values

4

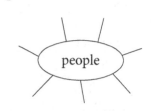
people

6 Which word from the box can precede every word in each group of words below? Use your dictionary to help you decide and check any meanings you don't know.

| advertising | ~~brand~~ | consumer |
| market | retail | shopping |

EXAMPLE: awareness, image, leader, loyalty, name

  brand (brand awareness, brand image, etc.)

a goods, issues, products, rights, society

b bag, basket, centre, mall, spree, trolley

c agency, budget, campaign, executive, slogan

d forces, leader, niche, research, segment, share, value

e business, outlet, price, therapy

7 Which of these expressions take *right*, which take *wrong* and which can take either? Delete the words which *don't* apply. Use your dictionary to help you and check any meanings you don't know.

EXAMPLE: bark up the *right/wrong* tree

a be in the *right/wrong*

b be the *right/wrong* way round

c be within your *rights/wrongs*

d catch somebody on the *right/wrong* foot

e do the *right/wrong* thing

f get hold of the *right/wrong* end of the stick

g get on the *right/wrong* side of

h get out of bed on the *right/wrong* side

i rub somebody up the *right/wrong* way

j strike the *right/wrong* note

k start off on the *right/wrong* foot

l the *rights/wrongs* and *rights/wrongs* of something

m two *rights/wrongs* don't make a *right/wrong*

Use of English

8 Read the text below. Use the word given in capitals at the end of some of the lines to form a word that fits in the gap in the same line. There is an example at the beginning (0).

One woman in five is a shopaholic

'Retail therapy' – shopping to improve your mood – has become something of a fashionable leisure (0) ...*pursuit*... PURSUE in Britain in recent years. It is the acceptable face of something much more sinister – the serious medical condition of shopping addiction. The number of people suffering from this illness has (1) .... the TAKE number of drug and drink addicts combined. Some experts believe that twenty per cent of the female population may be shopaholics. The condition has led to family break-ups, depression and (2) .... HOME

Psychiatrists claim one reason for the epidemic is that shopping has never been so (3) .... ALLURE Shopping centres are now beautiful, attractive places. In some shops, store cards or (4) .... cards LOYAL are offered indiscriminately at the till, and credit is still relatively easy to obtain. Experts also claim that shopping addiction often masks deeper problems. As one of them says, 'Mostly there is underlying depression and (5) .... , sometimes caused by a disturbed ANXIOUS relationship with one's parents. Cold and (6) .... parents often lavish presents on EMOTION their (7) .... , who then come to associate SPRING that with (8) ....' PLEASE

6 The sound of music

Listening

1 **04** You will hear a talk by a man called William Bond about his work as a freelance musician. For questions 1–9, complete the sentences with a word or short phrase.

William had some highly lucrative work at a local school, advising them about the (1) .... of students' playing or singing.

William likens the personal concerts he's given to the (2) .... that business people do.

William's most recent involvement with an opera production was as the (3) .... of the music.

An opera project for homeless people that William got involved in was paid for by (4) ....

The homeless people themselves indicated what they called the (5) '..' that William should try to capture in the music.

William says the work was hard for him, and likens the plot he had to work with to a (6) ....

William says the opera featured many different types of music and made him see (7) .... music in a new light.

When talking about the opera's themes, William says one of the contributors sings about imagining himself in a (8) ....

The background compilation accompanying some water songs featured a (9) .... which was praised by the audience.

Grammar

2 Complete this sentence in eight different ways by choosing the most appropriate ending (a–h) for each verb (1–8). Use each ending once only. You will need to think carefully about form and meaning.

EXAMPLE: *1 e He might practise in the music room with a bit of encouragement.*

He

1 might practise	a if he hadn't lost the key.
2 could've practised	b as we can't find him anywhere else.
3 should practise	c without first asking permission.
4 can't be practising	d as often as he can.
5 shouldn't have practised	e with a bit of encouragement.
6 must've been practising	f if his teacher hadn't recommended it.
7 might not have practised	g – he doesn't have his saxophone today.
8 must be practising	h or his things wouldn't still be in there.

(in the music room)

3 Complete these sentences using the verbs in brackets with an appropriate modal auxiliary from the box. You will need to think carefully about meaning and may need to change the form of the verbs. Sometimes you will need to use a negative. There may be more than one correct answer.

can	could	may	might	must	should

EXAMPLE: He *can't have enjoyed* (enjoy) the concert –
it was terrible!

a Research suggests you .... (score)
better on a standard IQ test if you listen to Mozart first.

b Strange as it .... (seem), Mozart's
music .... (have) a profound effect on
the brain.

c If you'd had a better violin teacher, you ....
(give up).

d Nobody was impressed by the musicians. They really
.... (prepare) better for the audition.

e If you're really interested in flamenco you
.... (go) to Spain.

f You .... (still learn) an
instrument, you know. It's not too late.

g I .... (say) I would go to the concert.
I'm really not looking forward to it.

h Nadia Gerber is listed twice in the programme. She
.... (play) in both pieces.

i Surely, they .... (both learn) the
trombone, can they?

j You .... (pass) your music exam if
you had practised a bit more.

k It's not very polite of him. He .... (let)
them know he was going to be late.

l The show .... (cancel) – it's
scheduled to run until December.

m She .... (practise) for an hour;
she only began 30 minutes ago.

n The technicians .... (set) the sound
system up wrong; we couldn't hear the strings at all.

o We were supposed to meet at the stage entrance after the
performance. Do you think he ....
(forget)?

p If you have been living abroad for three years, you
.... (hear) of him, but I can assure
you his music is very popular here now.

Vocabulary

4 One verb collocates with all the words and phrases (1–8) on the left. Use your dictionary to help you work out what it is and choose a meaning for each idiom you make from the definitions (a–h).

1 offence at
2 someone's advice
3 someone unawares
4 pity on
5 something lying down
6 the point
7 things as they come
8 some doing

a accept an argument
b deal with events calmly, as they occur
c surprise, startle someone
d be quite difficult
e feel hurt by
f follow a suggestion
g feel sorry for and help
h accept something without complaining

5 Complete each sentence with an adverb and an adjective from the box.

beautiful	~~cheerful~~	damaging
highly	obscenely	potentially
profitable	strikingly	
~~surprisingly~~	wealthy	

EXAMPLE: Considering they lost all
their possessions in the fire,
they are *surprisingly cheerful*.

a No wonder her daughter became
a model. She is ....

....

b Industry bosses are warning
that an interest rate rise now is

.... to
the economy.

c Some people think Hollywood's
top film stars are ....

....

d According to the latest annual
report, the company is actually

....

Use of English

6 Read the text below and decide which answer (A, B, C or D) best fits each gap. There is an example at the beginning (0).

EARPLUGS FOR ROCKERS!

Rock legends Phil Collins, Sting and Ozzy Osbourne all (0) ....A.... years of ear-blasting rock music have (1) .... their toll on their hearing. But a new European Union (2) .... introduced today means the likes of Morissey, Marilyn Manson and Madonna could all be sporting earplugs onstage as they churn (3) .... their greatest hits. While the image perhaps isn't very rock and roll, musicians have welcomed the new rules.

A spokesperson for the Musicians' Union said many artists, from orchestra players to rock stars, suffer hearing problems due to frequent (4) .... to loud music. 'We welcome the new legislation and are calling on all musicians to (5) .... in custom-made earplugs.'

The rules (6) .... pubs, nightclubs, restaurants and concert arenas, all of whose management must now ensure the hearing of their staff is protected if music in the venue regularly (7) .... 85 decibels. The regulations do not, however, (8) .... to members of the public.

0	**A** claim	**B** mention	**C** hold	**D** demand
1	**A** made	**B** taken	**C** set	**D** paid
2	**A** legislation	**B** directive	**C** command	**D** notice
3	**A** over	**B** away	**C** out	**D** back
4	**A** presentation	**B** vulnerability	**C** outlook	**D** exposure
5	**A** invest	**B** purchase	**C** secure	**D** acquire
6	**A** comprise	**B** incorporate	**C** relate	**D** cover
7	**A** exceeds	**B** overtakes	**C** passes	**D** transcends
8	**A** utilise	**B** address	**C** apply	**D** spread

7 Read the text below and think of the word which best fits each gap. Use only one word in each gap. There is an example at the beginning (0).

The early years of MTV

The popular TV music channel MTV was launched in 1981 in the US **(0)** ......*with*...... the intention of playing **(1)** .... but music videos. It was a brilliant marketing concept, as it came at little cost while **(2)** .... extremely attractive to record companies and advertisers.

The videos were guided by an air-host known as a VJ – the term is a conflation of 'video' and 'disc jockey'. The VJs are now a **(3)** .... of the past, but **(4)** .... their heyday, they *were* MTV, attaining cult status. It was **(5)** .... presenters on the station that Russell Brand and Alex Zane got their first career breaks.

MTV changed the way we experience music: we watched records instead of just listening to them. Record companies were quick to appreciate this, and acts such as Madonna and Boy George, **(6)** .... appeal was as much about their good looks **(7)** .... their music, went global. Such **(8)** .... the music video's impact that film directors at the height of their careers were attracted to the medium.

8 Read the text below. Use the word given in capitals at the end of some of the lines to form a word that fits in the gap in the same line. There is an example at the beginning (0).

The *Other* Mozart

Everyone has heard of Wolfgang Amadeus Mozart; few of his musical son Franz Xaver. A new CD collection **(0)** ......*entitled*...... *The Other Mozart* celebrates Franz's | TITLE
music – in all its haunting, **(1)** .... innocence. The 27 songs are brief | MELANCHOLY
slivers of ideas, underdeveloped shadows of what might have been, reaching
a beautiful **(2)** .... in the later works. But it is clear that the music | FULFIL
never reaches the **(3)** .... of his genius father. | HIGH

Franz was the youngest of Mozart's children, and his mother's hopes and
ambitions focused on him following the **(4)** .... death of his father. | MATURE
The very best teachers were **(5)** .... available to Franz, who made | AUTOMATIC
his public debut as a singer, aged five. The songs bring to light Franz's pianistic
accomplishment; the piano parts are extremely demanding. The songs hint at
Franz's love for a woman; they speak time and again of **(6)** .... | ATTAIN
love and unfulfilled **(7)** .... | LONG

(8) .... , however, the fact remains that this music, had it been | REALIST
written by a composer of any other name, would probably have remained buried
in the archives.

Reading

1 You are going to read an extract from an article about a popular TV cartoon series. Seven paragraphs have been removed from the extract. Choose from the paragraphs A–H the one which fits each gap (1–7). There is one extra paragraph which you do not need to use.

The Simpsons

Nick Griffiths meets the faces behind America's best-loved family of cartoon characters

Mike Scully, writer/producer of *The Simpsons*, is in Aspen Colorado with the show's creator, Matt Groening, to attend the four-day US Comedy Arts Festival. Among the attractions is *The Simpsons Live*, a read-through of two separate episodes on-stage by members of the cast.

| 1 |

The shorts ran from 1987 and were subsequently developed into a full series that made its début on American primetime two years later. From the off, the show was a huge hit, topping Fox's ratings. Although it is hard to figure out why it exploded so quickly, Scully has his own theory.

| 2 |

The Aspen venue for the *Simpsons* events is the Wheeler Opera House. The seven-strong cast take the stage, including Dan Castellaneta (Homer Simpson and others), Nancy Cartwright (Bart and others) and Yeardley Smith (Lisa).

| 3 |

Stripped of the visual distraction of animation, you also realise how relentlessly clever and funny the scripts are. After the show, Scully acknowledges, 'It's times like that when you realise just what an impact the show has had on people. *The Simpsons* were dysfunctional yet you could also see that they loved and stuck by each other. People have always liked that because they don't see enough of it in real life.'

| 4 |

Quite simply, *The Simpsons* redefined television animation, spawning shows that were extreme by comparison – which naturally helped its own acceptance into the mainstream. For every action, of course, there's an equal and opposite reaction. 'Every time there's a fad that kids really like, there's gonna be a grown-up going, "Something's wrong here"', says Groening. 'It happened with video games, heavy metal, rap, and Pokemon.'

| 5 |

Indeed, it was deemed so influential that even President George Bush Senior waded in, criticising its portrayal of the American family during his 1992 election campaign. His wife, Barbara, called the show the 'dumbest thing' she had ever seen.

| 6 |

Groening refers to his secret motto, 'To entertain and to subvert'. 'It's not so much trying to change the minds of people who are already set in their ways, it's to point out to children that a lot of the rules that they're told are by authorities who do not have their best interests at heart. That's a good lesson. Think for yourself.'

| 7 |

But perhaps what pleases Groening and Scully most is the well-known fact that families watch *The Simpsons* together. In an age of meals-on-the-move, three-television households, computer games and the Internet, it is an achievement of which they can be justifiably proud.

A Unwittingly, *The Simpsons* struck a chord, which endures today: however much they mess up and frustrate each other, they are a viable family unit. Yet the American networks misread this popularity as a public craving for more primetime animation. 'They rushed all these shows on air and the public rejected most of them,' Scully explains.

B 'At the core is a family, and everyone can identify with that,' he says. 'This is probably why it plays well overseas, too.' At the last count, the series has been shown in a staggering 94 countries worldwide.

C In a small way, *The Simpsons* probably contributed to the demise of the administration. 'It didn't fly with a lot of Americans,' recalls Scully. 'People who enjoyed the show didn't want to be told that they were watching something bad or stupid, or something wrong for their kids.'

D Serious issues crop up regularly on the show, cloaked in humour and vivid animation: corrupt media and politicians, ineffective policing, the environment. Groening again, 'In conceiving the show, I made sure Homer worked in a nuclear power plant, because then we can keep returning to that and making a point about the environment.'

E So a mere animation series has quietly subverted the world's youth, helped to bring down a president, been stamped all over what we wear and changed the face of contemporary animation. Now academics are using it in universities: 'Having the donut and eating it: self-reflexivity in *The Simpsons*' is part of the Introduction to Cultural Studies module at Edinburgh's Napier University.

F Groening is a chunky, bearded man with tiny specs, a floppy fringe, Simpsons baseball jacket and baggy jeans. Oregon-raised and LA-based since college, he initially conceived the Simpsons family as a brief animated segment within the new Fox TV network's *Tracey Ullman Show*.

G And such was the case initially with *The Simpsons*. Homer was seen as a disgraceful role model; Bart's insolence to his elders would encourage the same. Bart Simpson t-shirts (notably 'Underachiever and proud of it') became so popular that some schools banned them for their subversive messages.

H It doesn't matter that both episodes have been aired previously on television. In the second, Lisa falls in love with the school bully (Bart to Lisa: 'I'll probably never say this to you again, but you can do better'). Watching a short, smiling woman come up with his voice is surreal and deeply impressive.

Grammar

2   Complete these extracts with an appropriate participle form of the verbs in brackets.

While the No 1 Kodak box camera (**1**) .... (produce) in 1889 was a crucial landmark in the development of photography, two of the most significant cameras in terms of modern photography were the Leica 1, (**2**) .... (introduce) in 1925, and the Kine Exacta of 1937, (**3**) .... (consider) to be the forerunner of sophisticated SLR (single lens reflex) cameras. However, until the digital revolution swept all before it, it was the 1950s Hasselblad which became the most widely used professional 'work horse' camera, (**4**) .... (offer) as it did a wide range of specialist accessories. (**5**) .... (use) to capture the famous Apollo moon-landing pictures, the Hasselblad is also assured of a place in the history of photography.

One of the most dominant figures in photography, Henri Cartier Bresson's approach is that of the purist, (**6**) .... (use) the most basic equipment and never (**7**) .... (resort) to the contrivance of unusual viewpoints or exaggerated perspectives. (**8**) .... (study) painting, he took up photography seriously in 1931, (**9**) .... (go on) to exert a tremendous influence on the medium. He insisted that his pictures were not cropped and was at pains to preserve his anonymity. A phrase (**10**) .... (coin) by him to describe his own approach – 'the decisive moment' – has become the watchword for many thousands of photographers (**11**) .... (bend) on (**12**) .... (secure) a winning image.

Vocabulary

3 In each of the following sentences two of the words in italics collocate with the noun. Put a tick (✓) if the word collocates and a cross (✗) if it does not.

   a Clive has rather unusual *beady / blushing / bulging* eyes.

   b Maria has delightful *sparkling / twinkling / gleaming* eyes.

   c The man gave Clare a *fixing / menacing / piercing* look.

   d It was hard to tell what Jo was thinking because of the *bare / glazed / blank* expression on her face.

   e Adam was admitted to hospital suffering from *double / blurred / bloodshot* vision.

4 The words in capitals in these sentences are all anagrams of verbs meaning *see*. Use your dictionary to help you solve them. The first and last letters of each word are given.

   EXAMPLE: Try to p*icture* RUIPECT yourself lying on a beach in the hot sun.

   a I p...............d CREEVDIEP a note of unhappiness in her voice.

   b It's often quite hard to g...............p SRPAG what the professor is saying.

   c I can f...............e ESROSFE a time when everyone will use electric cars.

   d The new bridge is a sight to b...............d LOHDEB.

   e People who are colour-blind can't d...............h USTDHISINGI between red and green easily.

   f I was so surprised when he turned up – I'd v...............d DALEUVSISI someone much older.

   g I thought I g...............d MDSIPGLE a shadowy figure at the window of the old house.

   h When do you e...............e VENGESAI finishing the project?

   i He couldn't c...............e OCCENIVE of a time when he would not be able to paint.

Use of English

5 Complete the second sentence so that it has a similar meaning to the first sentence, using the word given. Do not change the word given. You must use between three and eight words, including the word given.

   1 It is absolutely essential to get this parcel off today or we will lose the contract.

   despatched

   This parcel ....

   fail or we will lose the contract.

   2 Central Gallery is nowhere near as good since there was a change of ownership.

   downhill

   Central Gallery has really ....

   hands last autumn.

   3 When I was young, cycling 80 kms a day was easy, but I couldn't do it now.

   difficulty

   In my ....

   cycling 80 kms a day, but I couldn't do it now.

   4 Sarah's mother complained constantly but Sarah didn't pay attention any more.

   notice

   Sarah no .... complaining.

5 Geoff is unlikely to be invited to the wedding as he appalled everyone with the way he behaved.

doubtful

In view of his ....

be invited to the wedding.

6 They were playing so well, there was no way they would lose the final match.

bound

Such was the standard of .... the final match.

6 Read the text below and decide which answer (A, B, C or D) best fits each gap. There is an example at the beginning (0).

Marcel Marceau, the mime artist

Wearing white trousers and a striped vest, and with a **(0)** ..D.. mask of a face, the celebrated mime artist Marcel Marceau produced a whole **(1)** .... of unforgettable characters – waiters, sculptors, matadors and ballet dancers. One critic said of him 'He **(2)** .... in less than two minutes what most novelists cannot do in volumes.'

As a child in the 1920s Marcel enjoyed the silent movies of the time, learning from the **(3)** .... of Buster Keaton and Charlie Chaplin how to express your feelings **(4)** .... mime.

Marcel toured the whole world doing his mime show based on the antics of 'Bip', the character he created. The names Marcel Marceau and mime became **(5)** .... linked in the public mind and the Japanese in particular **(6)** .... under his spell. Marcel also appeared in several films, including Mel Brooks's original *Silent Movie*, in which Marceau spoke the only line – **(7)** .... the only audible word – 'Non!'

The list of Marcel's prizes and honorary doctorates is enormous, and the city of Paris has a permanent mime school **(8)** .... after him.

0 A typical	**B** truthful	**C** precise	**D** veritable
1 A host	**B** gathering	**C** multitude	**D** swarm
2 A fulfilled	**B** attained	**C** accomplished	**D** executed
3 A equals	**B** likes	**C** counterparts	**D** parallels
4 A through	**B** across	**C** under	**D** by
5 A inextricably	**B** irretrievably	**C** infallibly	**D** irrevocably
6 A ran	**B** fell	**C** stood	**D** lay
7 A likewise	**B** indeed	**C** similarly	**D** furthermore
8 A entitled	**B** called	**C** termed	**D** named

8 Urban jungle

Listening

05 1 You will hear three different extracts. For questions 1–6, choose the answer (A, B or C) which fits best according to what you hear. There are two questions for each extract.

Extract One

You hear two people talking about city life.

1 What does the man say about the location of his childhood home?
  A It still retains some of its appeal.
  B He appreciates more than ever how excellent it was.
  C People comment on it in a sentimental way.

2 What does the woman imply about her country?
  A There is no ideal part to live in.
  B People in it have a cynical attitude.
  C The countryside is preferable to the towns.

Extract Two

You hear two people talking about a city hotel.

3 The woman suggests that the hotel management
  A believe in keeping a very low profile.
  B are much more ruthless than first appears.
  C do relatively little to improve its state of repair.

4 What does the woman say about the staff?
  A Their politeness is fake and over the top.
  B They are well known for giving slow service.
  C Not all of them are honest and reliable.

Extract Three

You hear two people talking about a problem with cars in a local street.

5 The speakers agree that the problem with cars in this street
  A encourages people to cheat the system.
  B produces a distinctly strange situation.
  C causes a lot of confusion even among locals.

6 What do the speakers see as the real source of the problem?
  A Residents' parking spaces aren't fixed.
  B Non-residents are free to park there.
  C Too many permits are handed out.

Use of English

2 Read the text below and think of the word which best fits each gap. Use only one word in each gap.

Civilisation and Urbanisation

Early civilisations, as (1) .... to merely primitive early societies, seem to have a common positive characteristic in (2) .... they change the human scale of things. They bring together the cooperative efforts of large numbers of people, usually bringing them together physically in large agglomerations.

Civilisation is usually marked by urbanisation. It (3) .... be a bold individual who was willing to draw a precise line at the moment when the balance tipped towards a dense pattern of agricultural villages clustered (4) .... a religious centre or a market to reveal the first true city. However, it is perfectly reasonable to say that more than (5) .... other institution the city has provided the critical mass which produces civilisation.

Inside the city, the surpluses of wealth produced by agriculture (6) .... possible other things characteristic (7) .... civilised life. They provided for the upkeep of a priestly class which elaborated a complex religious structure, leading to the construction of great buildings serving more than merely economic functions, and in due (8) .... to the writing down of literature.

Use of English

3 Read the text below and decide which answer (A, B, C or D) best fits each gap. There is an example at the beginning (0).

Urban gum crime

The Mayan tribes of South America would chew chicle, a natural form of rubber, while the Ancient Greeks (0) ....A..... the resin of a mastic shrub. In modern Britain, we like to chew sticks and tablets of manufactured gum – and (1) .... of the tasteless sticky residue on the ground.

However, recent legislation in the UK means that used chewing gum is now (2) .... as litter and anyone who drops it on the pavement or (3) .... in any public place is committing a crime and can be fined. Some areas have council litter wardens who can (4) .... on-the-spot fines.

A new government campaign (5) .... the extent of the problem and aims to (6) .... awareness about this anti-social habit, for instance with posters in shopping areas. Throughout the UK, councils spend £150m a year removing chewing gum from the streets, and £4m of that is in London alone. Indirectly, this is (7) .... taxpayers' money. (8) .... is the main removal method, but use is also made of chemical sprays, freezing, pressurized water and steam.

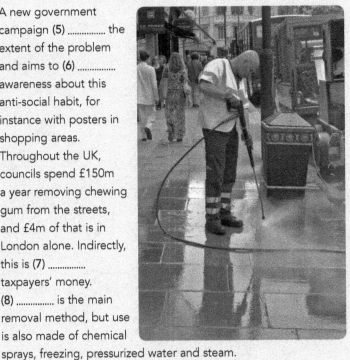

0	**A** favoured	**B** approved	**C** commended	**D** indulged
1	**A** discard	**B** dispose	**C** dispense	**D** disperse
2	**A** ranked	**B** classified	**C** systematised	**D** codified
3	**A** at any rate	**B** anyway	**C** even so	**D** indeed
4	**A** fix	**B** compel	**C** impose	**D** prescribe
5	**A** features	**B** declares	**C** focuses	**D** highlights
6	**A** make	**B** provoke	**C** grow	**D** raise
7	**A** no doubt	**B** for sure	**C** of course	**D** within reason
8	**A** Scraping	**B** Clawing	**C** Scratching	**D** Rubbing

Grammar

4 Rewrite these sentences starting with the word(s) given.

EXAMPLE: The minute the mayor walked into her office, the phone started ringing. (No sooner)

No sooner had the mayor walked into her office than the phone started ringing.

a The traffic ground to a halt just after they joined the freeway. (Scarcely)

b The council only started showing interest in the redevelopment scheme last month. (Not until)

c These are by far and away the most imaginative proposals the city has ever received. (Never before)

d Government investment in public transport is often not remotely adequate. (Seldom)

e The new transport network had not long been open when a number of similar schemes were announced in cities around the country. (Hardly)

f The only other time I have seen such deprivation was in slums that are now demolished. (Only once)

g It is very difficult for town centre redevelopments to achieve a harmonious balance between old and new. (Rarely)

h After the minister had finished his tour of inspection, he made his pronouncement. (Only after)

5 Rearrange these words to make meaningful sentences containing an inversion. The first two words of each sentence are correct.

   EXAMPLE: Around the core city's boulevard a fine intact medieval runs wide.
   Around the city's intact medieval core runs a fine wide boulevard.

   a So stressful becoming more and more are seeking city life that alternatives is people.
      So stressful ....
      alternatives.
   b Under no take own circumstances matters residents their should into hands.
      Under no ....
      hands.
   c Little was mayor to signed by was land desk a petition 50,000 people on his aware the that about.
      Little was ....
      desk.
   d On no property developers account will you everything tell believe should you.
      On no ....
      you.
   e Not only further on the way already unemployment a problem also losses job was were but.
      Not only ....
      way.
   f In no to jeopardise the scheme did they want of the success way.
      In no ....
      scheme.
   g Not one the development councillor accepted to observe the invitation.
      Not one ....
      development.
   h Little did demolition work so quickly and neither did she expect the to start I.
      Little did ....
      I.

Vocabulary

6 Rearrange the words in bold to complete the sentences.

   a 'Racism **in place no has** football,' said the team manager.
   b I'm sick of living with my parents. I just want **my place own of a**.
   c I don't think you should come in here, sonny. This is **for place a no** child.
   d '... and with that record-breaking swim, Jennifer Davies has earned herself **history a in place**,' said the commentator.
   e He can be difficult to get on with, but **his right the heart's place in**.
   f I'm not really bothered about that cookery course. You can **my go place in** if you want.
   g The whole course has been a disaster! I wish I'd never agreed to do it **the in place first**!

7 Use words from the box to complete the useful phrases with 'place'.

change	fall	hold	lose
save	take (× 2)		

a Keep your finger on the line you're reading, then you won't .... **your place**.

b Will you .... **me a place** in the queue – I just need to go and get something else.

c If you will kindly .... **your places**, ladies and gentlemen, dinner will be served shortly.

d Can I .... **places with** you so I can get a better view?

e 'Hmm, I'm starting to understand,' said the detective. 'Everything's beginning to .... **into place**.'

f Here, just .... the wood **in place** and I'll screw it in.

g Marcie will .... **the place of** Susan, who's unfortunately fallen ill.

8 Take a word from the first box and a word from the second box to complete these compound adjective collocations. The first one has been done for you.

deep	~~densely~~	labour	long (× 2)
money	slow	world	

famous	making	moving	~~populated~~
rooted	saving	serving	winded

a	densely	populated	area
a		-	fear
a		-	pianist
a		-	explanation
a		-	device
a		-	vehicle
a		-	member of staff
a		-	venture

9 Complete these extracts with nouns from the boxes.

air	burden	departure	flow
hour	offers	road-users	
standards	transport		

After little investment in infrastructure for 25 years, California's (1) .... system is groaning. The situation is so bad that businesses complain about potential employees turning down job (2) .... that would require them to spend several hours a day driving. Car makers are also concerned. They worry that the poor (3) .... quality in California's suburban areas will mean they are ordered to meet impossibly strict design (4) .... to reduce pollution.

Road-pricing has long been championed by economists, keen to impose more of the external costs of driving on (5) .... by charging them a fee that reflects not just the distance travelled but also the time and route of the journey. Commuting imposes a heavier (6) .... when it is done at rush (7) .... so such journeys ought to cost a driver more. In theory, drivers will then adjust their (8) .... times and smooth out the (9) .... of traffic through the day.

Reading

1 You are going to read an introduction to a book about clothes and fashion.
For questions 1–10, choose from the sections (A–D).

Which section

explains why non-mainstream fashion risks the possibility of social disapproval?	1
makes the point that fashion cannot be taken out of its historical context?	2
suggests a temporal link between wearing clothes and painting the body?	3
explains that certain clothes eventually become recognised as merely of historical interest?	4
suggests that someone might dress in a particular way in order not to attract attention?	5
suggests that clothes could be used to assert social standing?	6
mentions a fashion item which reflects a trend in society?	7
mentions clothes being put on in a very elaborate manner?	8
mentions satisfying one's own curiosity as a possible motive for dressing in unusual ways?	9
offers an explanation for the way in which dress codes originate?	10

THE SOCIAL PHENOMENON THAT IS FASHION

A Each day as we prepare to meet our world we perform a very popular ritual: getting dressed. This may mean only adding a daub of war paint or freshening a grass girdle. Or it may be the painstaking ceremonious robing of a monarch. For most of us, however, it means the exchange of nightwear for day clothes. Although nakedness does still exist in some isolated communities, there appears to be no society that is entirely composed of totally unadorned human beings. The desire to alter or to add to the original natural state is so prevalent in the human species that we must assume it has become an inborn human trait. When did it begin? It certainly precedes recorded history. Bodily covering was probably the first man-made shelter and the human skin the earliest canvas. Standing erect with his arms and hands free to function creatively, man must have soon discovered that his anatomical frame could accommodate a wide variety of physical self-improvements. His shoulders could support a mantle to protect him from the elements. To stand out above his peers and indicate his superior position, he found his head could be an excellent foundation for adding stature and importance. Intertwined with these motivating factors and building on them was the human instinct for creative expression, an outlet for the aesthetic spirit.

B Changes in needs and outlooks often blur the purposes that originally gave articles of human raiment a raison d'être. Vestiges are relegated to tradition; others undergo a kind of mutation. The sheltering mantle, for example, can become a magnificent but cumbersome robe of state. Amulets, their symbolism lost or forgotten, become objects of decoration to show off the wearer's wealth. Man is a gregarious creature. And although innovations and changes may be initiated by individuals, the inspiration that triggers them grows out of the innovator's environment, and their acceptance or rejection is determined by his society. Nothing so graphically reflects social and cultural patterns as the manner in which individuals within a society alter their original appearance.

C Fashion can be a powerful force. Societies evolve for themselves a set of rules, and most people, consciously or subconsciously, do their best to conform. The nonconformists, those who do not wish to join in this game, must either sever their relationship and go it alone or suffer the consequences. These regulations are hardly capricious. Their roots are in the foundation of a society which, although composed of individuals, develops an identity of its own and an instinct for self-preservation. A homogeneity in dress is a manifest catalyst, a visible unifier of a social group. Because this is so, costume if read properly can give us an insight not only into the class structure of a social organization but also into its religion and aesthetics, its fears, hopes and goals. Today our clothes continue to reflect our anxieties and how we try to cope with them. Our society is rapidly becoming global. The recent worldwide rage for jeans is an example of this new universality and the wholesale movement to break down past barriers – geographical and social.

D 'Fashion is the mirror of history,' King Louis XIV of France correctly observed. But if one were to transpose a fashion into another era, it would be unlikely to make sense. How, for example, could an Amazonian Indian or a Roman senator rationalize a hoop skirt, a starched ruff, or a powdered wig? Yet scrutinised through the specialist's lens, such vagaries of dress can help chart the course of social mores, moral codes, the march of science and the progress of the arts. This would explain why the genealogy of clothes receives the rapt attention of the psychologist, sociologist, economist, anthropologist and art historian, each posing the same question: 'Why do people wear what they wear?' Why, indeed, have human beings chosen to transform themselves so astonishingly? For the sake of the flesh or the spirit? For themselves and their own inquisitive nature or for the eyes of beholders? What has driven them? Ambition? Fear? Humility? There is and can be no single adequate response.

Use of English

2 Complete the second sentence so that it has a similar meaning to the first sentence, using the word given. Do not change the word given. You must use between three and eight words, including the word given.

1 Do you mind if I don't come back to the office after I've been to the dentist at lunchtime?
   afternoon
   Would you have any .... off after my dental appointment?

2 Everyone knows you are not allowed to smoke on domestic flights.
   ban
   It is common .... on domestic flights.

3 He knew nothing of his wife's impending promotion.
   about
   Little .... to be promoted.

4 He can't possibly have said anything like that.
   misheard
   You really .... completely.

5 All this media attention is quite unusual for a contemporary painting.
   receive
   Seldom .... much media attention.

6 Brian was offended when the teacher accused him of being disruptive.
   being
   Brian took .... disrupting the lesson.

Vocabulary

3 Which of these characteristics from the Chinese zodiac are negative? Use your dictionary to help you decide. Some may be a matter of opinion!

The Horse
athletic eloquent entertaining gifted hard-working independent quick-witted ruthless selfish unfeeling

The Goat
dissatisfied insecure irresponsible lovable peace-loving pessimistic sweet-natured undisciplined unpunctual

The Monkey
enthusiastic inventive long-winded passionate unfaithful untruthful untrustworthy witty

The Rooster
amusing boastful conservative extravagant industrious mistrustful pedantic pompous short-sighted vivacious

The Dog
courageous cynical devoted introverted modest noble prosperous respectable selfless stubborn

The Pig
gullible honest loyal materialistic naïve non-competitive scrupulous sensitive sincere sociable

4 Match the signs to these descriptions, underlining the characteristics in the table above that justify your answers.

EXAMPLE: They are funny, lively and hard-working, but they can also be a bit suspicious and self-important.

Rooster – amusing, vivacious, industrious, mistrustful, pompous

a Honourable, brave and well-to-do, they tend to attach easily to people and put others first, but they can be inward-looking and a bit obstinate.
b A bit innocent and easily taken in, they like the fine things in life and pay attention to detail. Very genuine, they enjoy being among people and will always stand by their friends.
c They are amusing, eager people who are good at thinking things up, but they can be unreliable and may not always tell the truth.
d They are kind and gentle people, easy to love, but not always easily pleased. They sometimes lack confidence, often have an underdeveloped sense of responsibility and can't always look on the bright side.

5 Add an appropriate prefix to make the opposite of these adjectives from exercise 3. Use your dictionary to help you.

EXAMPLE: *un*sociable

a ....enthusiastic   e ....noble
b ....honest   f ....selfish
c ....loyal   g ....sensitive
d ....modest   h ....sincere

6 Find the six compound adjectives in exercise 3 and use the *first* word of each to complete these sentences. Use your dictionary to help you. There may be more than one correct answer.

EXAMPLE: Some parents have a lot to put up with but are extremely *long-suffering*.

a The affair may have been very public but it was very ....-lived.
b The councillor's ....-hitting remarks at the meeting upset a lot of people.
c The Finance Director is renowned for being rather ....-tempered in a crisis.
d At election time, you will find ....-talking politicians everywhere.
e In any confrontation, her brother always adopts a ....-keeping role.

7 Which prefix can attach to every word in each list below? Use your dictionary to help you decide and check any meanings you don't know.

EXAMPLE: bearing, joyed, wrought
        over (overbearing, overjoyed, overwrought)

a conscious, literate, skilled
b disposed, eminent, possessing, occupied
c dated, going, raged, ranked, standing
d assured, centred, important, opinionated, satisfied, styled

Grammar

8 Use linkers from the boxes to complete these extracts. You will not need to use them all.

> at any rate   consequently   furthermore
> having said that   to some extent

Dear Mrs Livermore

Having investigated the matter, we are satisfied that no mistake has been made on our part. (1) .... I find that our sales staff have acted in a courteous and compliant manner. (2) ...., we are unable to agree with your request for a refund and further compensation. (3) ...., we will in the circumstances exchange the coat if you return it to the store within one week of this letter.

> all the same   even though   in brief
> on the contrary   what's more

Senior management are determined to push on with the policy reforms (4) .... everyone has pointed out several problems with these proposals. (5) ...., Mr Davies intends to go further than he has indicated in his email to all staff of 23 March. He claims that staff representatives have been 'obstructive and critical'; (6) ...., we believe we have acted in a positive, constructive manner.

> for that reason   in short   likewise
> on the whole

Anita has overseen a major acquisition, she has increased profits by thirty per cent, she has restored shareholder confidence in the firm. **(7)** .... she has transformed this company since she took over twelve years ago. **(8)** .... David has had a huge impact on the company since he arrived nine years ago.

9 Gerund or infinitive? Complete these sentences with an appropriate form of the verbs in brackets. There may be more than one correct answer.

EXAMPLE: They decided *to put off tidying* (put off / tidy) the house until their visitors had left.

a She stopped .... (iron) her clothes and started .... (put) them away.

b He regretted .... (take) the job when he found he couldn't stand .... (work) with his new boss.

c The new recruits all promised .... (improve) their standard of dress at work.

d Apparently, no-one minds her .... (be) so untidy round the house. Her housemates don't like .... (be) tidy themselves!

e They managed .... (defuse) the situation and .... (avoid / get) caught up in an ugly scene.

f We meant .... (practise / do) the yoga exercises but the director objected to us .... (use) the room.

g Having advised him .... (embark) on a course of therapy, the counsellor went on .... (suggest) that he try .... (see) a few different therapists before choosing one to work with.

h Until she heard his voice, she had forgotten .... (meet) him three years ago.

i 'Remember .... (stay) calm, whatever happens!' she shouted after him.

j You've let your house .... (get) in a terrible state. There's no point .... (try / clean) it yourself – you'd better .... (get) a professional cleaner in.

k I was hoping .... (buy) a new outfit for the occasion, but my parents have forbidden me .... (spend) any more money!

l Predictably, he denied .... (lie) to them about the theft.

m I've only found two things worth .... (read) in this newspaper.

n He's been meaning .... (phone) you for a couple of weeks now.

Listening

1 **[06]** You will hear part of a discussion programme in which a businessman called David and a linguist called Ivana are speaking about the theme of symbols. For questions 1–5, choose the answer (A, B, C or D) which fits best according to what you hear.

1 The view is expressed that brands should
   A symbolise something people enjoy.
   B seek to utilise something visually unusual.
   C learn to be more co-operative with each other.
   D represent more than just a business proposition.

2 When talking about globalisation both speakers agree that
   A the Internet has a huge influence.
   B the positive symbols outweigh the negative ones.
   C major sporting events are well-meaning but flawed.
   D people are right to take a benevolent view.

3 What point does Ivana make about language?
   A Some languages are particularly disposed towards symbols.
   B Writers use symbols in the same way as everyone else.
   C There is some debate as to what constitutes a symbol.
   D Speakers of a language use symbols without realising it.

4 What does David say about the symbol in his hockey team's name?
   A It should really be changed.
   B It's somewhat misleading.
   C It was initially misinterpreted.
   D It puts pressure on the team.

5 What do both speakers find absurd about colour symbolism and cars?
   A the idea that a red car is any easier to see
   B the notion of linking a driver's character with car colour
   C the contradictory arguments used by one insurer
   D the suggestion that insurers are influenced by cultural symbols

2 Recall these useful collocations and phrases from the listening by matching a word or words from Column A with one from Column B. The first one has been done for you as an example.

A	B
(to) project	icons
(to) update	controversy
commercial	belonging
a sense of	an image
cultural	transaction
political	a logo

[06] Check your answers by listening again to the recording.

Use of English

3 Read the text below and decide which answer (A, B, C or D) best fits each gap. There is an example at the beginning (0).

Saving Latin

Try telling the Reverend Reginald Foster that Latin is a dead language. The response will be an impassioned rant from a teacher who has dedicated a large (0) ...**B**... of his life to keeping the forerunner of the English and Romance languages alive. A man on a (1) .... , he speaks only in Latin to his students, (2) .... the language to life with his dramatic recitations.

But Reverend Foster is not alone. Latin plays a special part in Italian cultural heritage, and politicians and academics have (3) .... concerns that enthusiasm for Latin in schools appears to be on the (4) .... because of the popularity of English. Some purists even feel this is (5) .... their national identity. They have a point; in my experience Italians seem obsessed with using English words, and will (6) .... an English word into a sentence even when a perfectly good native word will (7) ....

But need we really fear for Latin just yet? Maybe not. Even if it is on its last (8) .... , it has survived for over 2,000 years.

0	**A** volume	**B** chapter	**C** act	**D** scene
1	**A** remit	**B** task	**C** vocation	**D** mission
2	**A** getting	**B** putting	**C** bringing	**D** setting
3	**A** conveyed	**B** voiced	**C** uttered	**D** sounded
4	**A** wane	**B** fall	**C** ebb	**D** drop
5	**A** deteriorating	**B** eroding	**C** disintegrating	**D** eating
6	**A** slip	**B** push	**C** cast	**D** post
7	**A** answer	**B** satisfy	**C** suffice	**D** content
8	**A** laughs	**B** leases	**C** lengths	**D** legs

4 Read the text below and think of the word which best fits each gap. Use only one word in each gap. There is an example at the beginning (0).

Plain English

WHEN CHRISSIE MAHER FOUNDED THE Plain English Campaign in 1979, little (0) ...*did*... she realise what a difference she would make to many people's lives. Exasperated by the complicated language of government forms and documents, Chrissie famously (1) .... hundreds of these to shreds in Parliament Square, London, and from (2) .... on the campaign began (3) .... earnest.

Chrissie knew she faced a difficult time persuading government departments and also big companies to use plain English. Luckily, she'd (4) .... an important lesson from her stunt in London – that publicity was a powerful tool. So she staged the first of her Plain English Campaign Awards. Trophies were given to organisations which communicate clearly and booby prizes to those (5) .... information was baffling. This (6) .... the desired effect, and recipients of booby prizes quickly rewrote their literature. Chrissie went (7) .... to demand clear information for consumer contracts, (8) .... many lawyers argued that rewriting legal documents in simple English could be unsafe.

The Campaign's standards are now recognised worldwide: their 'crystal mark' is a guarantee that a document is written in understandable English.

5   Read the text below. Use the word given in capitals at the end of some of the lines to form
    a word that fits in the gap in the same line. There is an example at the beginning (0).

Globalisation – a positive force

What is globalisation? **(0)** ....._Essentially_....., it means that today, more than ever before,   ESSENCE

groups and individuals interact directly across frontiers, without **(1)** ....   NECESSITY

involving the state. This happens partly because of new technology, and partly because

states have found that **(2)** .... is better served by releasing the creative   PROSPER

energies of their people than by restricting them.

The theoretical benefits of globalisation are obvious: faster growth, higher living standards,

new opportunities, but the problem is these benefits are very **(3)** ....   EQUAL

distributed and also the global market is not yet **(4)** .... by rules based   PIN

on shared social objectives. Thus the central challenge that we face today is to

(5) .... that globalisation becomes a positive force for all the world's people   SURE

instead of leaving billions of them in **(6)** ....   POOR

If we are to get the best out of globalisation, we must think **(7)** .... about   FRESH

how we manage our shared interests. That does not mean world government or the

eclipse of nation states. On the contrary, states can draw **(8)** .... from each   STRONG

other by acting together within common institutions based on shared rules and values.

Grammar

6   Complete these sentences with an appropriate
    form of the verbs in brackets. You will need to think
    carefully about form and meaning. Sometimes you
    will need to add *would*. There may be more than one
    correct answer.

a At times like this, I really wish we ....
    (speak) Japanese!

b She wishes .... (enrol) for a
    language course as soon as possible.

c I wish you .... (try) to
    get to grips with the Internet. I'm sure you
    .... (enjoy) it.

d If only the good things in life
    .... (be) free!

e I wish new technology ....
    (not keep) changing all the time.

f If only we .... (have) a mobile
    phone at the time, we ....
    (be able) to call them.

g She .... (pass) her exam last
    year, if only she .... (work)
    harder.

h He behaves as though he
    .... (be) the only
    caring person on the planet.

i If only globalisation .... (be)
    a positive force for all.

j If only we .... (not agree) to
    go with them that day.

k He was acting as though he ....
    (be) in a desperate hurry.

l Would you not rather they
    .... (seek) new sponsors than
    see the programme abandoned?

m It is time .... (start) taking
    the world's problems seriously.

n He wished more research ....
    (do) while the language still ....
    (have) speakers.

o I'd much rather you .... (ask)
    permission before helping yourself.

p They had hoped .... (move)
    the project on further before their funding
    .... (run) out.

Vocabulary

7 Complete this extract with nouns from the box.

development	emotions	forces	good	inequality	integration	standards	transport

The word 'globalisation' stirs powerful **(1)** .... Some see it as highly beneficial – a key to the future **(2)** .... of the world economy, more opportunities and higher living **(3)** .... across the world. Others see it as a malign force that increases **(4)** .... within and between nations, disempowers the weak, causes unemployment and increases poverty.

Most people agree that the **(5)** .... driving globalisation – technological change, lower communication and **(6)** .... costs, increased trade and financial **(7)** .... among countries – are powerful. But they need to be harnessed to make globalisation work for the **(8)** .... of all.

8 Make an appropriate phrasal verb or noun with *turn* for each picture by combining it with a word in the box. Use your dictionary to help you.

away	down	in (× 2)
off	out	over

a

EXAMPLE: *to turn somebody in*

....

b

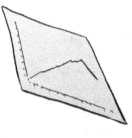

....

c

....

d

....

e

....

f

....

9 Complete these sentences, which all contain expressions with *turn*, using your dictionary to help you.

a Beside herself with emotion, she didn't know which .... to turn.

b Everyone agreed her redundancy was a very unfortunate turn of ....

c Goodness! You .... me quite a turn, creeping up like that!

d She is so kind. She'll do anyone a .... turn.

e It's bizarre. Since I joined the programme, I seem to meet him at .... turn.

f The coast road is so full of .... and turns, it's really quite dangerous.

Reading

1 You are going to read an article about relationship problems at work. For questions 1–6, choose the answer (A, B, C or D) which you think fits best according to the text.

FIGHTING TALK

It would seem that some people are simply incapable of settling scores amicably at work and practising some good old-fashioned forgiveness. A High Court judge was recently forced to order two doctors who were unable to settle a personal dispute to divide their surgery in two by building a wall right through their medical practice.

You might think that doctors Anne Rodway, 65, and Paul Landy, 49, were old enough to know better but somehow the two could not manage to work alongside each other. The two set up their partnership three years ago in Sevenoaks, Kent, but stopped talking just three months after their business started. Both staff and around 3,500 patients have been asked to decide on which side their loyalties lie as the practice is formally divided – especially difficult for the staff, who have already had to become used to being paid separately by the warring doctors.

Although an extreme case, it demonstrates just how bad things can get when communication and understanding break down between colleagues at work. Office feuds can be experienced in even the friendliest of environments. But what to do when faced with one?

Whether you are involved directly or an innocent bystander watching others curdle the workplace atmosphere, Jane Clarke, author of *Office Politics*, offers some sound advice. 'On the whole, people do not like dealing with conflict, but it is very important to grab the bull by the horns. If you feel you are able to, you should try and sort it out. If not, the very least you can do is report it to a manager who should make sure that workers know that bad behaviour in the workplace will not be tolerated.'

But what causes acrimony in the first place? Reasons can be as diverse as a clash of personalities, jealousy, backstabbing or a simple misunderstanding. If you are personally involved – and almost all of us have been in one way or another – then the best thing to do, says Clarke, is to try to put yourself in the other person's shoes. Easier said than done, since empathy is not an easy emotion to come by, even to the most virtuous.

'Often it is easy to dump on the other person and blame them totally for the situation but remember it is your problem and you have a responsibility to try to resolve it,' says Clarke.

Listening skills are vital. If the problem is between other colleagues, things can be a bit trickier. You may not be the gallant sort – practising an unhealthy dose of denial is often what most people would prefer to do – but ignoring the situation will not make it go away.

So what are your options? 'If you feel you are up to it, try talking with the feuding parties individually and try to understand what the issue is,' advises Clarke. 'Make it clear that it is not an acceptable state of affairs.'

Mediation is another option; get the two parties to sit together and act as a buffer zone. You might have the urge to bash their heads together, but it won't achieve a great deal. As Clarke says, 'Sometimes it is a case of translating. People are often so different that it seems that they speak a different language.'

Any meetings between disputing colleagues should have some follow-up. All involved should be made aware of the next steps – failing to do this could mean that the situation repeats itself.

Negative energy between people need not produce
66 bad karma. Harnessed creatively, it can actually become a positive force. So, if you are having problems with
68 office dullards who insist on putting downers on any bright new ideas you might have, use their criticism and
70 objections as a way of really testing a brainwave. Surely, if it can survive them, it can survive anyone. Try looking at people's weaknesses as strengths: assign a pedant to research the finer details of a project; the loudmouth of the office can always be pushed forward when it comes to public speaking.

Disputes and ill feelings can arise both among employees or between employee and employer, a fact clearly illustrated by the record numbers of people who contacted the conciliation service ACAS over the past year. Reassuringly, however, 76% of cases were settled through mediation – an indication, perhaps, that rather than working on building walls in the workplace, we should be bringing them down.

1 In telling the story of the two doctors, the writer suggests they
   A didn't give their partnership enough of a chance.
   B were totally incompatible from day one.
   C should have been able to resolve their problems.
   D were introverted and intolerant people.

2 What main point is the doctors' story used to illustrate?
   A Conflicts at work divide staff and clients.
   B The failure of relationships at work can have serious consequences.
   C Work conflicts can happen where you least expect them.
   D It is not always easy to know how to handle conflicts at work.

3 According to Jane Clarke, office disputes
   A occur for any number of reasons.
   B are caused in the first instance by acrimonious feelings.
   C are usually attributable to personality differences.
   D tend to arise when least expected.

4 The view is expressed that work conflicts will not get resolved unless both parties
   A have a personal involvement.
   B accept some blame for the situation.
   C commit to finding a solution.
   D accept each other in a spirit of friendship.

5 Which phrase from the penultimate paragraph sums up its main point?
   A bad karma (line 66)
   B harnessed creatively (line 66)
   C putting downers on (line 68)
   D testing a brainwave (line 70)

6 Which of the following best describes the tone of the article?
   A constructive and practical
   B detached and critical
   C understanding and empathetic
   D ironic and dismissive

Grammar

2 **Which of the adverbs in italics are correct? Sometimes both options are correct, sometimes neither option is correct. Delete the incorrect options and, if neither option is correct, suggest a suitable alternative.**

EXAMPLE: All three couples seemed ~~entirely~~ / *very* pleasant and ~~absolutely~~ / *eminently* suitable as foster parents.

a The new receptionist is *immensely / deeply* grateful to you for putting in a good word for her with her boss.

b There was something *deeply / absolutely* mysterious about her, which he found *extremely / rather* attractive.

c In this day and age, it is *utterly / entirely* unusual for couples to get married, let alone stay together 'till death them do part'!

d The line managers say the proposed pay rises are *woefully / fairly* inadequate and *grossly / greatly* unfair.

e New technology may be *absolutely / completely* marvellous, but developing a good working relationship with it can be *extremely / pretty* challenging!

f The new Finance Manager was *really / eminently* upset by the MD's remarks. We all felt they were *pretty / quite* hostile and not *entirely / mainly* reasonable.

g My new boyfriend finds my father *rather / utterly* intimidating, but Dad's actually *completely / quite* harmless.

h She's *highly / woefully* old now, but still *quite / really* determined to be independent.

i He's *fairly / absolutely* devoted to his cat. It's *utterly / immensely* hopeless trying to change him now!

Vocabulary

3 Which of the suffixes in the box can be used to make adjectives from these verbs and nouns? Use your dictionary to help you write in correct adjectives. Don't forget to indicate any possible negative forms using prefixes!

-able	-ary	-ful	-ible	-ical	-ive	-less	-ous	-some

a argue   *(un)arguable, argumentative*

b awe

c defend

d fear

e forget

f imagine

g moment

h rest

i sense

j use

4 Use adjectives from exercise 3 to complete these sentences.

EXAMPLE: At this stage, it is *arguable* which of them is more to blame for the problems in their relationship.

a It is quite .... how much some people are capable of achieving in life.

b She may have been extremely upset with him, but her behaviour was quite ....

c Starting a new life alone after years of marriage is a rather .... prospect for any new divorcee.

d I've noticed I'm becoming more and more .... these days. I must be getting old!

e We need to be sure that their grievances are real and not ....

f What do you think was the most .... discovery of the eighteenth century?

g Both parties were becoming .... waiting for the mediation proceedings to begin.

h That's utterly absurd. I've never heard anything quite so .... in my whole life!

i Sadly, their efforts to work out their problems were .... They've gone their separate ways.

5 Match these adverbs and adjectives to make appropriate collocations and use them to complete the sentences below.

blindingly	~~banal~~
comparatively	biased
deceptively	rare
heavily	obvious
highly	questionable
radically	simple
ridiculously	reformed
~~utterly~~	cheap

EXAMPLE: It was supposed to be a serious documentary programme, but the chatty approach was awful and made it *utterly banal*.

a It is .... whether these goals can be achieved within the time available.

b A book this old in such good condition is a .... find these days.

c The research they based on a so-called 'random' sample of couples turned out to be .... in fact.

d The test was .... : it looked much easier than it really was.

e It was .... to everyone, except it seemed to the manager herself, that the new proposals would not work.

f The 20th century saw many national institutions ....

g £25 is .... for something that normally costs £250 – there must be something wrong with it.

6 Correct the spelling mistakes that exam candidates made in these sentences, taken from the *Cambridge Learner Corpus*.

a This is a huge sacrifise that should be rewarded with respect and appreciation.
b I think this little story gives a good explaination of why people store useless objects.
c In the air it is possible to feel the happinness.
d I admire the strenght and courage of such people.
e If my wishes are not fullfilled, I am thinking of taking steps to go to court.
f The role of the computer in today's society is crusial.
g The media broadcast pictures of children like skeletons from malnutricion.
h This cottage with its special athmosphere helped us to forget about our problems.
i Since he played proffessionally in an orchestra, he was offered a scholarship.
j We became very fond of each other and nobody could separete us.
k Children are no longer inocent creatures waiting for their grandfather to tell them a story.

Use of English

7 Read the text below and think of the word which best fits each gap. Use one word only in each gap. There is an example at the beginning (0).

How on earth does she cope?

RICHARD EVENS has spent the last year surviving the wilds of Alaska living alone in a cabin in (0) ....order.... to 'discover himself'. It sounds fantastic, momentous and admirable – the only trouble (1) .... , he has a wife, Emily, and two children, all of (2) .... he has left behind. Emily has not seen her husband for the (3) ....

part of twelve months. So why on earth did she let him go?

Emily explains, 'Well, as (4) .... as I'm concerned, it's not a question of 'letting' him do anything. Marriage shouldn't hold you back. You see, in our marriage vows we said we'd support each other in our separate dreams as well as in our collective ones. And this was a

(5) .... in a lifetime thing for Richard. If he hadn't gone to Alaska, I couldn't have lived with that on (6) .... conscience. Being separated for a year is tough, but it's not as bad as having an unhappy husband. The time apart is a small (7) .... to pay if it means we get a better life at the (8) .... of it.'

8 Here are some more sentences about the same story. Complete the gaps in the same way.

a People often ask Emily what life's been .... without Richard.
b There is no doubt that Emily is .... good her promise to be supportive and, ... the difficult circumstances, she wouldn't have it any .... way.
c 'When we decided to go .... with the idea, it made perfect .... for me and the kids to move back to Scotland to be near my own parents.'
d 'We didn't want to stay in our old house in England. .... we done that, Richard's absence would've been more keenly felt.'

12 At the cutting edge

Listening

1 **07** You will hear five short extracts in which different people are talking about the Internet.

TASK ONE

For questions 1–5, choose from the list (A–H) what each speaker's attitude is towards the Internet.

Attitudes

A frustrated by the way it invites misuse

B enthusiastic about its potential

C sceptical of claims about its safety

D indifferent to its existence

E intolerant of its triviality

F concerned about the speed of its development

G puzzled by its complexity

H accepting of its drawbacks

Speaker 1   **1** [ ]

Speaker 2   **2** [ ]

Speaker 3   **3** [ ]

Speaker 4   **4** [ ]

Speaker 5   **5** [ ]

TASK TWO

For questions 6–10, choose from the list (A–H) what each speaker currently uses the Internet for most.

A research for work

B pursuing a personal hobby

C checking financial details

D completing a piece of work

E making a future arrangement

F doing a favour for somebody

G contacting a colleague

H making purchases

Speaker 1   **6** [ ]

Speaker 2   **7** [ ]

Speaker 3   **8** [ ]

Speaker 4   **9** [ ]

Speaker 5   **10** [ ]

Grammar

2 Complete the sign explanations below using an appropriate verb from the box in the passive with a modal if necessary. There is sometimes more than one correct answer.

extinguish   keep   ~~leave~~   ~~park~~   permit   remove   reserve   switch off   wear

EXAMPLE: Cars *may be parked* free of charge but vehicles and their contents *are left* entirely at the owners' risk.

a Eye protection .... at all times.

b All cigarettes .... before entering this area.

c All fire exits .... clear and free of rubbish.

d Mobile phones .... before entering this concert hall.

e No unauthorised persons .... beyond this point.

f This space .... for disabled parking only. Unauthorised vehicles ....

3 Read the text and look at the words in bold.

Article

search

What Causes Motion Sickness?

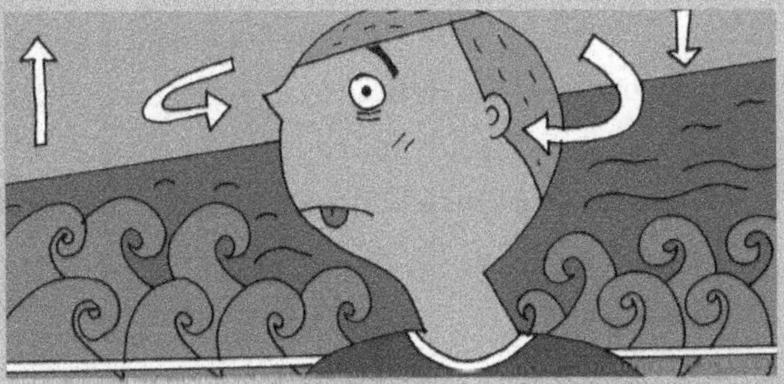

Motion sickness is caused by repeated motion such as from the swell of the sea, the movement of a car, or the motion of a plane in turbulent air. In the inner ear, which is critical for detecting motion, this **affects** our sense of balance and equilibrium and, hence, our sense of spatial orientation. The symptoms include nausea, vomiting and dizziness.

The symptoms appear when the central nervous system **receives** conflicting messages. The brain **senses** motion through three different pathways of the nervous system that send signals coming from the inner ear, the eyes and the deeper tissues of the body surface.

When the body is moved intentionally, for example when we walk, our brain **coordinates** the input from all three pathways. When there is unintentional movement of the body, as occurs during motion when driving in a car, the brain is not coordinating the input, and we **think there is** discoordination or conflict among the input from the three pathways. We **hypothesize** that the conflict among the inputs is responsible for motion sickness.

The distressing symptoms of motion sickness usually stop when the motion that causes it **ceases**. However, there are people who suffer symptoms for even a few days after the trip is over. One common suggestion is to simply look out of the window of the moving vehicle and to gaze toward the horizon in the direction of travel. This **reorientates** the inner sense of balance by providing a visual reaffirmation of motion. A simple remedy is chewing, which **reduces** adverse effects of the conflict between vision and balance.

Where there is a verb in bold in the text above rewrite the phrase or sentence to make it passive. The first one has been done as an example.

a affects ... *our sense of balance and equilibrium are affected, and*
b receives ...
c senses ...
d coordinates ...
e think there is ...
f hypothesize ...
g ceases ...
h reorientates ...
i reduces ...

Vocabulary

4 Hidden in the box are 12 verbs. To find them you need to look horizontally → and vertically ↓. One has been done for you. When you have found them all, think of one verb which they could all be said to mean.

A	Z	S	D	H	A	C	K
H	S	L	I	C	E	H	S
S	A	I	S	I	C	O	E
S	W	T	S	K	U	P	V
L	A	C	E	R	A	T	E
A	E	X	C	I	S	E	R
S	O	H	T	I	P	L	B
H	O	I	N	C	I	S	E
P	T	R	I	M	W	Y	S

5 Complete these sentences using each verb from exercise 4 once. You may need to change the form of the verb.

EXAMPLE: The man's face was severely *lacerated* in the accident.

a A programmer has managed to .... into some top-secret government data.

b He .... open the envelope with a knife.

c My hair grows so fast, it needs .... again already.

d In biology classes at school we used to .... rats.

e The museum was broken into by vandals again last night and several paintings were ....

f Could you .... me a very thin piece of cake?

g The design is .... into a metal plate.

h She's .... and changed jobs for as long as I've known her.

i He was .... away at his violin, making a terrible noise!

j Although his hand was completely .... , surgeons have been able to sew it back on.

k During the operation, the surgeon .... several tumours from the wall of the patient's stomach.

6 Complete these sentences with the appropriate adverb particle or preposition. There may be more than one correct answer.

EXAMPLE: Apparently he was really cut *up about* the research grant being withdrawn.

a It's time this engine had a service. It keeps cutting ....

b They were hoping a good talking to would cut her .... size.

c Although she came from a wealthy family, she was cut .... without a penny.

d It's a problem that seems to cut .... all strata of society.

e As funds start to get low, we may have to cut .... lab time.

f He doesn't think twice about cutting .... , no matter who you are talking to.

g The bandage was so tight it was starting to cut .... the circulation.

h Have you finished cutting .... the templates yet?

i She was so angry she cut the cheque .... lots of little pieces.

j Three more trees would have to be cut .... before the site was cleared.

k It's quicker if you cut .... the park.

l There's an awful lot of red tape to cut .... before we get the project up and running.

7 Use the nouns from the box to complete useful idiomatic phrases highlighted in bold. There is one noun that you will not need to use.

| buttons | edge | fuse | machine |
| screw | test | wavelength | years |

a Camaneta has his opponent at his mercy, and now he's really **turning the** ....

b Here at JBB we're **at the cutting** .... **of** pharmaceutical research.

c Professor Jakes is very hard to talk to; I'm not quite sure I'm **on the same** .... as her.

d Maria's department runs like **a well-oiled** ....

e Don't do anything to upset Mr Appleby – he's got rather **a short** ....

f Shamanova ran well in Budapest two weeks ago, but **the acid** .... **of** her ability will be the European Games next month.

g I'm afraid I think companies like Ravelli are **light** .... **ahead** of us in terms of research and development.

8 Unscramble the words in brackets to complete useful idiomatic phrases.

a Barcelona have had a decent start to their season, but you sense they're not yet .... (all firing cylinders on).

b You'll be fine in your algebra test, don't worry! .... (it's science not rocket)!

c Look, I'm sorry to .... (spanner the put works in a), but I really don't think this proposal is going to work.

d I think Roger will get the job. He's young, enthusiastic and he .... (the buttons all right pushes).

e Nadal played brilliantly in the first two sets, but rather .... (out ran of steam) later in the match.

f I hope that's clear, but just .... (the hammer point to home), let me show you one last slide.

Use of English

9 Read the text below. Use the words given in capitals at the end of some of the lines to form a word that fits in the gap in the same line. There is an example at the beginning (0).

Just how **(0)** ...... *readable* .... should a popular science book be? This may seem an odd question, but   READ

there is an important issue at stake here. This was made clear at the Aventis Science Book Awards, when jury

chairman Lewis Wolpert **(1)** .... espoused the cause for making the genre more demanding   PASSION

of readers. The biologist believes too many science writers are now running scared of **(2)** ....   COMPLEX

As he points out, the public does not expect great **(3)** .... figures like James Joyce or   LITERATE

T.S. Eliot to be easy to follow. Indeed, readers positively relish their intricate styles. So why then do we not

have such **(4)** .... of science writers?   EXPECT

Wolpert's belief is **(5)** .... by his jury's choice of winner – Brian Greene's long,   EXAMPLE

dense and extremely technical *The Elegant Universe*, a singularly **(6)** .... treatise on   COMPROMISE

cosmology. But how far should one go down this route? Although elegantly written, the book is so dense and

opaque that it pushes the notion of popular science writing close to the precipice of **(7)** ....   COMPREHEND

and leaves one fearful that it will only daunt, rather than attract, the **(8)** ....   INITIATE

10 Complete the second sentence so that it has a similar meaning to the first sentence, using the word given. Do not change the word given. You must use between three and eight words.

1 Research scientists are having to carry out too many administrative tasks.

required

Research scientists are .... much of an administrative role.

2 He's done something very brave that most men wouldn't be capable of doing.

takes

It .... what he did.

3 You'll never believe how marvellous the Great Pyramid is unless you see it.

seen

The Great Pyramid has .... believed!

4 Grant's tutor told him he had too many scientific terms in his presentation.

cut

Grant's tutor told him .... of scientific terms in his presentation.

Save the planet

Reading

1 You are going to read a newspaper article about an eco-trip to South Africa. Seven paragraphs have been removed from the article. Choose from the paragraphs A–H the one which fits each gap (1–7). There is one extra paragraph which you do not need to use.

Blooms with a view

Mike Herd explores the fynbos, a region of South Africa that shows a way forward when an eco-system is fragile

For five days and nights in February 2006, the fire blazed a 50-mile trail from the outskirts of Cape Town down towards Africa's southernmost point. Then, unexpectedly, the wind changed direction – meaning workers and fire staff at the Grootbos Private Nature Reserve stood no chance against the flames. Conference guests had to be hurriedly evacuated before the lodge complex was completely engulfed. So how come Grootbos's chief botanist, Sean Privett, is smiling as he recalls that dramatic incident? 'Hey, they were just buildings, they could be rebuilt,' he says with a grin. 'But this was also a whole new opportunity for rare plant species to germinate and flourish. We found something like 70 new species here in the months after the blaze.'

1 [ ]

Sean, we discover, is not the only person around here who is fanatical about flowers. This beautiful stretch of South Africa's Western Cape, known as the Overberg, may be a prime spot for watching whales and great white sharks, but for many of its landowners the priority is protecting the proteas, orchids, ericas and carniverous sundew plants (to name but four of the region's floral families) which make up the fynbos – shrubland with as rich an array of plant species as you'll find anywhere on the planet. Grootbos's conservation efforts began 20 years ago, when Heiner Lutzeyer and his son Michael bought the original 123-hectare farm, and Heiner started photographing and documenting its indigenous flora.

2 [ ]

These days, the reserve stretches to some 1,750 hectares. And while guests are treated to the height of five-star luxury – including what may be the world's finest view direct from a bathtub – it is clear that conservation, including a strong commitment to educating and employing workers from the poorest local communities, remains the primary concern in what the Grootbos website calls 'this botanic wonderland'.

3 [ ]

Fortunately, in addition to beach horse riding and whale watching, Grootbos also lays on a trademark 'flower safari' to introduce guests to the most striking flora on the reserve. And today we're lucky enough to have Sean and his battered old Jeep guiding us. First question, then: what's the floral equivalent of seeing a lion?

4 [ ]

As we try to follow Sean's identifying yells, bright flashes of colour and scent assault us from all directions. Among them delicate pinks and yellows of little erica plants, heather-like flowers that at the right times of year bathe whole valleys in a pink, yellow or white wash. No two neighbouring plants, it seems, are ever allowed to hail from the same species. It's as if the fynbos has been designed by a mad botanist who's been overdoing it on the organic fertiliser.

5 [ ]

By the end of the safari, I've lost count of how many weird and wonderful species we have encountered – from spectacular crimson candelabra flowers that detach and roll along with the wind, to the orange-flowered and not-at-all-potent wild marijuana plants. In danger of joining the ranks of the florally obsessed myself, I ponder out loud why there should be quite so many different species of plant here.

6 [ ]

These conditions are also proving increasingly attractive to winemakers, who reckon tricky soils produce more interesting wines because the grapes have to work harder. But rather than proving an irritant to local conservationists, the neighbouring Lomond wine estate belongs to the region's pioneering 'biodiversity and wine initiative', which pledges to protect rare and endangered plant species by only using sustainable farming methods.

7 [ ]

Almost everyone, it seems, understands the fragility of the ecosystem here – and with good reason. One recent report counted the Cape Floristic Region as among the 10 places in the world most threatened by climate change: a predicted temperature rise of 1.8°C over the next 40 years would spark a dramatic increase in the number of wildfires like the one that did so much damage in 2006. The eco equation says the fynbos needs fire to flourish – but not too often, or it will be wiped out entirely.

A Suddenly there's a yell from deep in the undergrowth which sends birds scattering into the sky. 'Over here!' Sean shouts, pointing at a large and slightly sun-withered white flower guarded by tall, bright pink spikes. 'King Protea, the biggest of all the Protea family and the national flower of South Africa ... here's that defining moment you were after.'

B But it isn't always the case. One such species, the Moraea lurida iris, only ever appears here immediately after fire has cleared the landscape of all the other, more bullish, plant species. Sean delights in showing us these beautiful, deep purple flowers emerging across the hillside – and describing the scent of rotting meat they give off to attract flies for pollination.

C Then, like a proud parent, he opens his arms to the dense shrubland around him: 'With the exception of our ancient milkwood forest, you can say that all the plants here were born on the same day.'

D 'It's hard to put your finger on it,' Sean says, disarmingly. 'There are so many factors ... the lack of any ice ages; all the different types of nutrient-poor soil; the weather systems rolling up from Antarctica; and the fact this region has never been farmed intensively. It's just a really unusual mix.'

E Of the six completely new species that have since been discovered here, two – Lachenalia lutzeyeri and Capnophyllum lutzeyeri – have been named after him ... not bad for a man with a purely amateur interest in botany.

F Graciously, Sean offers no hint that this inquiry might be unworthy of one of South Africa's foremost botanical experts. Instead, at the highest point of the Grootbos reserve, he yanks on the handbrake and bounds off into the middle of the knee-high shrubland. I have to admit, though, that what appears uniformly green from a distance is anything but when you are in the thick of it.

G Likewise, the nearby Flower Valley Farm, which grows indigenous fynbos plants for the cut-flower trade, is run by a public conservation trust which ensures that neither the fynbos nor local workers are exploited for profit.

H All very admirable too, but there's just one thing ... I daren't mention this to Sean but, following our hour-and-a-half's drive down from Cape Town through dustbowl-dry arable fields, I'm feeling a little confused. We have been greeted by a stunning mountainous coastline, certainly – but not quite the explosion of floral colour I'd been expecting. Rather, it's a plainish green moorland. Can we really be in the heart of the smallest but most precious of the world's six designated floral kingdoms, with – according to my guidebook – species far outnumbering those found in the entire Amazon rainforest?

Grammar

2 Use these frameworks to rewrite the quotes below in reported speech. There may be more than one correct answer.

EXAMPLE: A leading conservationist says …
(that) one of the greatest challenges facing the future of rhinos in both Africa and Asia is maintaining sufficient conservation expenditure and effort in the field.

a Industry consultant William Moore acknowledged .... , but said ....

b Harold Barrington, a recycling enthusiast from Oklahoma, said .... He claimed .... Apparently, he ....

c Liz Newman, a mother of three, mused .... and she sometimes wondered .... She concluded ....

d Recycling specialist David Dougherty questioned .... , when .... He insisted .... He reckoned .... In his view, people .... But they ....

EXAMPLE:

One of the greatest challenges facing the future of rhinos in both Africa and Asia is maintaining sufficient conservation expenditure and effort in the field.

Recycling paper will never completely eliminate cutting down trees, but it could mean cutting fewer trees.

I've built a machine that makes petroleum out of old tyres. I've produced as much as 8,000 litres of crude oil in five hours. I distilled some into gasoline to run my machines and sold the rest to a refinery.

We live in a world surrounded by concrete and sometimes I wonder what I can do about the environment. Well, I can at least sort my trash.

Why cut down a tree to make a newspaper with a lifetime use of just over 20 minutes, then bury it? You can use it six times over, then burn what's left to create energy. We've got to make recycling a natural part of the economy so that it becomes a part of our lifestyle. Of all the environmental concerns that have come up through the years, this is the most personal. People are uncertain what they can do about saving whales or the rain forest. But they can recycle their waste every day of their lives.

Vocabulary

3 Match a word from the left with a word from the right to make some common strong collocations that are useful for talking about the environment. There may be more than one correct answer. Use your dictionary to help you.

1	energy	**a**	disaster
2	renewable	**b**	development
3	ecological	**c**	nations
4	soil	**d**	action
5	drought-stricken	**e**	consumption
6	industrialised	**f**	waste
7	worst-case	**g**	energy
8	sustainable	**h**	areas
9	concerted	**i**	scenario
10	radioactive	**j**	erosion

4 Complete each sentence with a synonym of the word in brackets. Some letters have been given.

a The d_v _ _ _ _ _ _ n (destruction) of the world's rain forests is a real cause of concern.

b The council has given its full b_ _ _ _ _g (support) to the new flood defence proposals.

c I do wish people wouldn't just c_ _ _k (discard) litter in the street.

d In East Africa we saw the terrible sight of children suffering from m_ _n_ _ _ _ _ _ _n (starvation).

e When cloud particles become too heavy they fall to the earth as p_ _c_ _ _ _ _ _ _n (rainfall).

f Kangaroos and koalas are both i_ _ _g_ _ _ _s (native) to Australia.

g In this highly fertile region, water is in a_ _ _d_ _t (plentiful) supply.

5 Complete the sentences by changing the root word given in bold. The first one has been done as an example.

diverse

a In the rainforest we witnessed astonishing biological ....diversity............. .

b The company intend to .... into new areas.

conserve

c Obviously, energy .... is high on our agenda.

d My brother is a .... and works on many interesting environmental projects.

human

e The loss of the forest has important implications for ....

f Following the disaster, ... aid is pouring into the country.

pollution

g Plastic is a major ....

h The company will fulfil its agreement not to .... the nearby river.

active

i Political .... clashed with police in the capital city.

j You can .... the entry system to the protected zone by voice recognition or a password.

consume

k .... of fossil fuels rose by 6%.

l Of course, the costs are indirectly borne by the ....

donate

m The charity rely exclusively on .... from the public.

n I'm a regular blood ....

Use of English

6 Read the text below and think of the word which best fits each gap. Use one word only in each gap. There is an example at the beginning (0).

Large areas of the famously wet country called England, notably in the south-east, have had very low rainfall for the (0) ....best.......... part of two decades. In one recent year, England's rainfall was less than any country in Europe (1) .... than Belgium and Cyprus. Less, (2) .... is, than the national average in famously dry countries like Spain and Portugal. And yet, English people expect their kitchen taps, (3) .... fail, to deliver, in 30 seconds flat, a litre of ex-river water from which (4) .... trace of human and animal sewage, pesticides and fertilisers, has been removed. They expect, and get, (5) .... of the best quality tap water in the world – as much of it as they want, as (6) .... as is required.

Even the British government seems to regard the country as a kind of gigantic, inexhaustible sponge. The water industry gazed in dismay as plans were finalised to build another 200,000 households in London, one of the driest parts of the country, (7) .... the course of the next ten years. Yet extraordinarily, the water companies were not consulted (8) .... after the expansion plans had been published.

Listening

1 〔08〕 You will hear part of a programme in which a coach called Rob Johnson and a physiotherapist called Donna Davies are discussing health and fitness. For questions 1–5, choose the answer (A, B, C or D) which fits best according to what you hear.

1 When asked about the best sport for fitness, Rob says that
   A more research is needed to reach a definitive answer.
   B it all depends on the proficiency of the participant.
   C even he is no longer certain on this issue.
   D no two people will give the same answer.

2 When talking about what constitutes fitness, Donna says that
   A a new theory can be discounted.
   B she's aware of seeming contradictory.
   C the answer is much simpler than people imagine.
   D a popular misconception exists.

3 Both speakers regard 'cross training' as
   A unnecessary for most people.
   B a misleading name for what it achieves.
   C counter-productive for serious athletes.
   D something that can stress the body too much.

4 What does Donna say about gyms?
   A Some users would do better to go elsewhere.
   B The variety they offer can provide motivation.
   C They enable people from different sports to learn from each other.
   D Some of them encourage false expectations.

5 On the issue of whether fitness is related to good health, the speakers agree that
   A there is surprisingly little evidence to support this.
   B it's possible to take too much exercise.
   C this is true regardless of a person's age.
   D unfit people are by definition unhealthy.

2 〔08〕 Listen again and complete these expressions from the recording.

   a a sprint swimmer **is an entirely different** .... **from** a distance swimmer

   b if you're a serious cyclist then **it's a moot** .... whether you'll benefit from going off and doing some rowing

   c your feet and legs really .... **a battering**

   d swim too much and the sprinter will lose some .... **bulk**

   e cross training .... **to be effective if** it ...

   f uses **a highly** .... **motion** that isn't actually natural at all

   g over-..................... **yourself** can no doubt lead to lowered resistance to infection

   h So **it's** .... **and roundabouts** really.

Grammar

3 Circle the correct preposition or particle and insert the appropriate article (*a, an, the,* or – if no article is required) in the gaps. There may be more than one correct answer.

a .... research carried out by .... Institute of .... Respiratory Medicine *at / in* .... Royal Prince Alfred Hospital in Sydney, Australia, suggests that there is .... correlation *between / with* the consumption of oily fish and .... reduction *in / of* children's risk *at / of* developing .... asthma. New studies are also beginning to make .... connection *between / with* a deficiency in .... omega 3 fatty acids and .... depression and .... mental illness.

b Jane Clarke is .... state-registered dietician and .... author *for / of* the *Bodyfoods* series of .... books. As .... teenager she was interested in medicine but wanted to work *by / with* food instead of .... drugs, so she did .... degree *in / of* dietetics *in / at* Leeds University.

c Everyone responds differently *to / with* food in the morning: some people feel sleepy and unable to function after eating .... large breakfast, whereas others need .... hearty breakfast before they embark on .... day's activities.

d .... chocolate causes your blood-sugar level to rise quickly, which stimulates .... pancreas to produce .... insulin, ... hormone that rapidly brings it *down / under*. .... fresh fruits give .... best slow-release energy boost, so increase your fruit intake.

e .... strenuous exercise results *in / to* .... release *of / with* .... endorphines in .... brain, giving athletes .... natural 'high'. Some athletes become dependent *on / to* .... effect, but it does not harm them *in / by* any way.

f Make sure that you drink plenty of .... water throughout .... day to enable all .... energising vitamins, minerals and slow-release sugars in the food that you eat to be absorbed *by / through* your body. .... adults should aim to drink two to three litres of .... water .... day.

g It is best to exercise every day. Three days .... week is .... absolute minimum. Work out .... best time of .... day to fit in .... exercise programme. It is unwise to exercise if you are injured or if you have any form of .... fever or .... viral infection such as .... cold or .... flu.

Vocabulary

4 Replace the verbs in italics with a more neutral verb that has the same meaning and fits in the sentence. There may be more than one correct answer. Use your dictionary to help you.

a The new manager came with a reputation for *shirking* his responsibilities.

b The relay team would continue *striving* for the record.

c Pedro *pleaded* for another chance to play for the team.

d The coach has *shunned* them completely since they *resigned from* his club.

e Francesca *resolved* to *confront* them about the missing equipment.

f The player walked off the pitch *clutching* his injured arm.

g We *trawled* through the programme to find out when we were competing.

h Lara always was one to *relish* a challenge!

i It seems they *trounced* the competition to cross the finish line in record time.

j This afternoon, Arsenal will *bid* to become Champions for the first time in eight years.

k The government has *pledged* more money for health promotion.

l Jean *addressed* a large audience of health professionals.

m I was advised to *eliminate* sugar completely from my diet.

n Marta's bad foot will *compromise* her ability to compete in athletics this season.

o My sports physiotherapist *advocates* the use of resistance bands.

p Martin *alleged* that he'd been fouled on the edge of the penalty box.

q The coach refused to *disclose* how much he was paid last year.

r The French town of Lyon *boasts* incredible sports facilities.

s Exercise is vital in the battle to *combat* heart disease.

t I cannot *conceive* how anyone can swim as far as that!

5 Using the clues in the picture and your dictionary, complete the sentences with an appropriate idiom. (The number of missing words is given in brackets.)

EXAMPLE: These training shoes cost *an arm and a leg*! (5)

a After worrying about the problem for two months, she was glad to .... (5)

b Could you come back later? I'm .... in work at the moment. (4)

c The thought of diving from the high board .... (6)

d She's an amazing swimmer. She's .... the others at the club. (4)

e I'm .... today. That's the third time I've dropped my chart. (4)

f Did you really win the marathon or are you just .... ? (3)

g Working with people half my age certainly helps to .... ! (5)

h This application form defies the imagination – I can't .... it at all! (4)

i It takes the coach hours to get the sports hall ready, but the players never .... to help him. (3)

Use of English

6 Complete the second sentence so that it has a similar meaning to the first sentence, using the word given. Do not change the word given. You must use between three and eight words, including the word given.

1 Very few contestants entered the race when it was first run.

   handful

   The race was contested .... first year.

2 Dawn has the potential to become a great tennis player.

   makings

   Dawn .... a great tennis player.

3 I'd hoped to stay in bed a bit longer than normal, but the phone rang.

   paid

   The phone ringing put .... a lie in.

4 Like many teenagers, Beth started disliking sport because she was self-conscious about her body.

   account

   Like many teenagers, Beth took a .... self-conscious about her body.

5 The agreement was that if I lent you the money you'd pay it back by Friday.

   understanding

   I lent you the money .... be paid back by Friday.

6 If Monica never speaks to him again he's got what he deserves.

   another

   If Monica never says .... him right.

7 Read the text below and use the word given in capitals at the end of some of the lines to form a word that fits in the gap in the same line. There is an example at the beginning (0).

An astounding achievement

As a teenager, Joe Decker was an **(0)** ....overweight.... couch potato. He   WEIGH
devoured beer, pizza and cookies and saw his weight balloon. When he
joined the US army, he could barely run two miles and had to endure the
(1) .... of extra training in the 'fat boy programme'.   HUMILITY

Yet the same Joe Decker has recently been named the world's fittest man
after completing the most gruelling physical challenge on earth in a record
time. Scarred by **(2)** .... jibes about his weight, 30-year-old   END
Decker is now enjoying the title, bestowed on him by Guinness World
Records, of 'Workout King of the World'. Where once he had layers of
(3) .... blubber, now he has lean, honed muscle.   WANT

Guiness spokesperson Chris Sheedy said: 'His achievement is momentous,
(4) ...., superhuman. We were initially sceptical about his   BELIEF
claims, but he sent us videos, eyewitness **(5)** .... , doctors'   STATE
reports – more evidence than we needed to **(6)** .... his claim.'   VALID

However, all this has come at a cost. Decker has experienced hallucinations,
(7) ...., dehydration, tunnel vision and extreme   ORIENT
(8) ....   TIRE

Reading

1   You are going to read an article about gender and the division of labour. Seven paragraphs have been removed from the article. Choose from paragraphs A–H the one which fits each gap (1–7). There is one extra paragraph which you do not need to use.

Men can't help it; blame their biology

In an ideal world men would be women. They would be home-makers and child-minders, cooks and cleaners, unabashed by wearing an apron. They would even use those 'baby-changing stations' that now forlornly decorate public toilets in airports and motorway service areas.

1

Which is not say the new man does not exist. You see him toting the baby on his back, or filleting the kiwi fruit for his partner's supper. However, the new man's most salient characteristic is his rarity. If he had feathers, he would be an endangered species.

2

So, are men just behaving badly? Or is there another reason why they shy away from the iron? Ironing a shirt does not call for extraordinary skill, and men living on their own manage it perfectly well, so why do they shrink from the duty when they are married?

3

'Men are more susceptible to boredom,' says Professor Marvin Zuckerman, an expert on neurotransmitters. 'What happens when you don't get variation stimulation? What happens when there is nothing changing, nothing novel? It's an unpleasant feeling. Not quite anxiety or depression, dissatisfaction. Men are more impatient and, when they're bored, they find different ways to express their boredom.'

4

Except, of course, for the problem of serotonin. 'It all became routine, mundane, boring. You start to feel: "I did that yesterday, so why should I do it again today?" And then you start to think, "Well, I won't do it today. I'm not bothered today." And then it just deteriorates from there.'

I think a nine iron for this one...

PUGH

5

The differences are visible in brain-scans. When a man does a crossword puzzle, only the left side of his brain is active, but a woman's brain lights up like Blackpool. She uses both sides of her brain while she solves the clues. And what is true of verbal challenges is true to much of life. Studies show that, in general, the male's brain is focused while hers is more integrated.

6

Last year an experiment was set up to test Fisher's findings. Six men and six women were challenged to complete a series of tasks in a limited time. They had to wash up, brew coffee, make toast and scrambled eggs, iron a shirt and take a phone message. The result was a walkover for the women.

7

Kevin and Lisa finally declared their experiment a failure. 'When Kevin went back to work it was as though a burden had been lifted, he was so chirpy,' Lisa says. Kevin feels he is back doing what he should be. 'We get on much better now I'm at work because I come home and I'm satisfied for the day. I've done my work, I've done a good job,' he says. So you can be a new man, if that is what you want – but only by undergoing a sex change. Easier, perhaps, to wear an unironed shirt?

A 'The female's brain is architecturally designed to do several things at once, whereas the male brain is more focused, more compartmentalised, more built to do one thing after another,' says Helen Fisher, an anthropologist who is also studying the brain. 'And, of course, the home is a place where you need to do a lot of things all at once – like clean the loo, answer the telephone, defrost the peas, feed the dog, change the baby and iron the shirts.'

B Biology, that's why. The culprit is a neurotransmitter called serotonin. We all have it in our brains, but men have less of it, and the less serotonin you have the more impatient and impulsive you are. Serotonin acts as a braking system on our impulses. It placates. It permits us to endure routine and boredom. And men are serotonin-challenged.

C All surveys of household responsibilities show that men are stubbornly resistant to their new role as house-husbands, though interestingly the newer the relationship the more pliant he is. But once he has his boots firmly under her table he becomes the old brute once again – only two per cent of men in stable relationships help with the washing and ironing.

D It's not hard to imagine – there's no financial reward and there's certainly no glamour; there's precious little job satisfaction and not much to look forward to from one day to the next except more of the same. But the role of the housewife is different today and, more importantly, so are society's attitudes towards it.

E Take Kevin Beck and Lisa Bates. They fell in love. They married. Each was on their second marriage and each had two children and, because Lisa was on a fast-track career, they agreed that Kevin would be the house-husband. 'I've always looked after myself,' he says, 'and I thought that I could manage. I'm pretty tidy so I thought the house would be as neat and tidy as I want it. I thought it should be a breeze.'

F And it is not just multitasking. Studies also show that from early childhood males have a greater tolerance for dirt. They do not see the stains on a bath or the dust on the bookshelves. Males also have a different sense of smell. He does not detect many of the pheromone-related odours (smelly socks, sweaty shirts) of which women are acutely aware. He sees sweetness and order where she sees filth and decay.

G However, as men cannot be women we have had to settle for the next best thing: the 'new man'. His specifications were dreamt up by feminists who rigorously refuse to recognise any innate differences of aptitude or attitude between the sexes.

H The house got messier as Kevin's low boredom threshold rebelled. Blouses got burnt instead of ironed as his brain strayed in search of diversions. However it was not only serotonin that was crippling Kevin's good intentions. The brains of the male and female are organised in different ways, and this organisation is not an accident of upbringing or culture – it is hard-wired into the cells from conception.

Vocabulary

2 Complete the sentences using linkers from the box.

despite	conversely	indeed
by the same token	likewise	
whereas	on the other hand	

a David seemed to favour the first interview candidate, Miss Stokes, ... Susan clearly preferred the third, Mr Allen.

b David clearly favoured Miss Stokes. .... , he refused to consider anyone else.

c David said, 'Miss Stokes scored highly on personal presentation. .... , she was not so impressive at organisational skills.'

d David said, 'I'm not sure about Mr Allen's honesty. Some of the things he mentioned were not on his application form, and .... some of the information on his form was never mentioned.'

e David said, 'Miss Stokes seemed very friendly to me. .... the second candidate, Mr Robson was highly approachable.'

f David said, 'Susan, you're criticising my choice, Miss Stokes, for being slow to answer some questions, but .... I could say that your choice, Mr Allen, was quite abrupt when he answered me.'

g .... David's concerns, Mr Allen was offered the job.

3 Unscramble the words in brackets to make useful idioms and neologisms.

a I don't know the exact projected amount, but we can say £15 million as
.... (figure ballpark a).

b I'm getting really fed up ....
(the fingers working to my bone) for no reward!

c As you know the economic outlook isn't great. In fact
.... (all and gloom doom it's).

d I'm sorry, there's nothing I can do. My boss has ruled on this and
.... (tied my are hands).

e The company's doing OK, just OK. At least we're managing to
.... (our water keep above heads).

f He's renowned for being a creative thinker. He's very good at
.... (the outside box thinking).

g Everyone in this department seems to be getting a bit complacent! Well,
.... (it's for check a time reality).

h It's all very well for Mr Cooper to make vague promises. He needs to
.... (put where his money mouth is his).

Grammar

4 **Match the two halves of these sentences.**

1 She left the office by the fire escape
2 She didn't leave until she'd cleared her desk
3 She really needed a back-up plan
4 She phoned to tell them she'd be late for the meeting
5 She found it difficult to clear out her hard copies

a **in case** things didn't work out the way she wanted.
b **for fear that** she might be discarding something important.
c **so as to** avoid having to confront her boss.
d **so that** items of low priority could be addressed in her absence.
e **so as not to** walk in on a backlog the next morning.

5 **Complete the sentences with a phrase from the box. More than one answer may be possible.**

for fear that	in case	in order to	in order not to
lest	so that	so as to	so as not to

a He went into work early on Monday ....
schedule things and do some planning.

b He was desperate to hide his mistake from his boss
.... it would jeopardise his promotion.

c He needed input from everyone in the department
.... make the wrong decision.

d He kept photocopies of all his important documents
.... there was a computer crash.

e He made a point of working through his breaks
.... he would impress his boss.

6 **Look again at the last sentence. How many other ways can you complete it?**

He made a point of working through his breaks **in order to ...**
He made a point of working through his breaks **in case ...**
He made a point of working through his breaks **for fear that ...**
He made a point of working through his breaks **so as not to ...**

Use of English

7 Read the text below and decide which answer (A, B, C or D) best fits each gap. There is an example at the beginning (0).

NEVER TOO OLD TO START A BUSINESS

It's not just budding young entrepreneurs who start up new businesses. Fifty-year-old Jane Owers, from London, has left her job in education to make her **(0)** ....A.... as a florist. Jane believes she **(1)** .... a better chance of success than someone half her age, as she has life experience and financial collateral in the form of property. As she explains, 'It's often the fear of financial failure that **(2)** .... others from starting up on their own. With me, it was more of a **(3)** .... risk. If the worst **(4)** .... to the worst, I can always **(5)** .... my losses and return to my previous profession. Hopefully, though, that's just a worst-case **(6)** ....'

Jane's business plan was a modest one. Her bank manager was **(7)** .... over by her realistic outlook and convinced that with Jane there would be no rash or self-indulgent spending **(8)** .... As a result he was happy to loan her the money she needed.

0	**A** mark	**B** stamp	**C** niche	**D** sign
1	**A** represents	**B** supports	**C** holds	**D** stands
2	**A** deters	**B** avoids	**C** curbs	**D** cautions
3	**A** figured	**B** calculated	**C** weighed	**D** gauged
4	**A** gets	**B** takes	**C** comes	**D** puts
5	**A** cut	**B** count	**C** let	**D** lift
6	**A** situation	**B** eventuality	**C** occurrence	**D** scenario
7	**A** won	**B** charmed	**C** swept	**D** caught
8	**A** binges	**B** sprees	**C** revels	**D** feasts

16 Hidden nuances

1    **09** You will hear five short extracts in which different people are talking about trying to write their first novel.

TASK ONE
For questions 1–5, choose from the list (A–H) how each person felt during the experience.

A frustrated by lack of progress

B worried about being seen as controversial

C cut off from real life

D stressed by time pressure

E reluctant to depart from a plan

F limited by a personal shortcoming

G unhappy about one section

H aware of being unoriginal

Speaker 1 | 1 |

Speaker 2 | 2 |

Speaker 3 | 3 |

Speaker 4 | 4 |

Speaker 5 | 5 |

TASK TWO
For questions 6–10, choose from the list (A–H) what each person learnt.

A be more concise

B keep revising what you write

C don't put too much of yourself into the work

D don't do anything too experimental

E create interest at various moments

F don't write if you're not feeling inspired

G don't underestimate your ability

H leave some things to the reader's imagination

Speaker 1 | 6 |

Speaker 2 | 7 |

Speaker 3 | 8 |

Speaker 4 | 9 |

Speaker 5 | 10 |

2 Here are some other snippets said by the speakers (but not on the recording). Form a word in each gap from the word in brackets.

a I didn't expect to create a
.... (literature)
masterpiece at my first attempt!

b I think hard about both the literal and
.... (figure) meaning of
the words I use.

c I was aware that what I'd written was
.... (contradict)

d When reviewing my own first drafts, I always
look out for any ....
(consistent) in the argument.

e I was told to .... (person)
what I was describing, rather than merely
reporting it objectively.

f I was delighted to be told that my sub-plot was
woven .... (seam) into my
main storyline.

g I was told my novel scored highly on
.... (create).

h Now all I have to do is sit and wait for the
.... (publish) date of my
book!

i I freely admit I absolutely cannot write
.... (describe) passages!

j I realise that when I get writing I have a
.... (tend) to ramble.

k I was told to make sure I aroused the
.... (curious) of the
reader.

l I kept on remembering the words of my old
English teacher: '...................................
(character) is everything.'

m I think one of my ....
(strong) as a writer is ....
(portrait) character.

n I was delighted to be told I'd created a highly
.... (atmosphere) novel.

Grammar

3 Choose the most appropriate option in italics to make sentences that are grammatically correct and meaningful. Sometimes both options are correct.

a *Despite / Even though* she has a wonderful turn of phrase, she finds it impossible to write good fiction.

b *However / As* acclaimed the novel is, it is not always totally accessible.

c *Although / Whereas* he has written hundreds of poems, he has only had two anthologies published so far.

d *Despite / Much as* I enjoyed the autobiography, I thought it could have been shorter.

e Talented *as / though* he is, he has not yet managed to finish a single story.

f *As well as / As a result of* writing short stories, she also writes poetry.

g *Even though / However* powerful a phrase may be, it should never be used for its own sake.

h *As / Though* dramatic *as / though* her plots are, they are not terribly original.

i *Whereas / As* novels can range from around 150 to 1000 plus pages, short stories must conform to far stricter length constraints.

j *As well as / In spite of* several rejections, he has just had his first volume published.

k *Despite / In spite of* public expectations, the novel did not win the award.

l *In spite of / As a result of* their successful screenplay, they were approached by other film companies looking for scriptwriters.

m *As / Much as* I have already indicated, everyone thinks they can write fiction.

n *Although / As* adjectives certainly have their place in creative writing, they should never be overused.

o *Much as / However* I would love to be a writer, I know I don't have the self-discipline.

p *As / Whereas* I have hinted, poetry is not for me.

Vocabulary

4 Complete the sentences with the words in the box, which are all to do with things being hidden.

camouflaged	concealed	covert
disguised	encoded	invisible
lurking	masked	obscured
secret	shrouded	veiled

a It looked like a blank sheet of paper, but there was a message on it in .... ink.

b The .... lighting in the room was very effective and extremely tasteful.

c Many satellite broadcasts are .... so that they can only be received by people who have paid to see them.

d Two new skyscrapers had sprung up and .... the view from her window.

e As I walked down the street I thought I saw someone .... in the shadows.

f Suddenly two .... gunmen burst into the shop and demanded all the cash in the till.

g Her reason for confessing to a crime she never committed remains .... in mystery.

h The murdered soldier belonged to an army unit that specialises in .... operations.

i The troops had .... themselves so effectively that the enemy didn't notice them approaching.

j How dare you come in here issuing .... threats like that?

k Who sent you those flowers – have you got a .... admirer?

l In the book the author gives a thinly .... account of his own early teaching experiences.

5 Underline the silent letter in each of these words.

answer	country	indict	receipt
business	debt	island	rhyme
circuit	gnome	listen	salmon
column	handkerchief	marriage	yeoman

6 Complete this poem with words from the box. You will need to think carefully about sound, spelling and meaning.

bead	bear	bird	both	broth
cart	choose	dead	dear	debt
dough	font	go	heard	meat
mother	rose	there	through	
ward	word	work		

I take it you already know
Of tough and bough and cough
  and (1) ....
Others may stumble, but not you
On hiccough, thorough, bought
  and (2) ....
Well done! And now you wish, perhaps,
To learn of less familiar traps?
Beware of (3) .... , a dreadful word
That looks like beard and sounds like (4) ....
And (5) .... : it's said like bed, not
  (6) .... –
For goodness' sake don't call it 'deed'!
Watch out for (7) .... and great and threat.
(They rhyme with suite and straight and (8) ....)
A moth is not a moth in (9) .... ,
Nor (10) .... in bother, (11) .... in brother,
And here is not a match for (12) .... ,
Nor (13) .... and fear for
  (14) .... and pear.
And then there's dose and
  (15) .... and lose –
Just look them up – and goose
  and (16) .... ,
And cork and (17) .... and
  card and (18) .... ,
And (19) .... and front and (20) .... and
  sword,
And do and (21) .... and
  thwart and (22) ....
Come, come, I've hardly made a start!
A dreadful language? Man alive!
I'd mastered it when I was five.

Use of English

7 Complete the second sentence so it has a similar meaning to the first sentence using the word given. Do not change the word given. You must use between three and eight words including the word given.

1 Despite her disappointment at his decision, Karen did not think badly of him.

bore

Although she ....
feelings over his decision.

2 Whether I read for ten minutes or two hours, the result is always a headache.

end

No matter how ....
with a headache.

3 John's been behaving badly ever since he befriended Colin.

friends

Ever since John ....
a turn for the worse.

4 I always end up crying in romantic comedies, however funny they are.

fail

However funny they are, romantic comedies ....
tears to my eyes.

5 At night, our neighbours would always keep their cat in for fear it would get run over.

case

At night, our neighbours' cat used never ....
run over.

6 Having three children to look after every day had taken its toll on Elke.

grind

Elke was worn ....
looking after three children.

Reading

1 You are going to read a newspaper article about global optimism. For questions 1–10, choose from the sections (A–D). The sections may be chosen more than once.

In which section does the writer

exemplify how short-term gloom tends to lift?	1
mention a pessimistic forecast that is nothing new?	2
express his hope that progress is not hindered by bad decisions?	3
acknowledge trying to find common ground with those who would oppose him?	4
point out directly how money needs to be invested?	5
suggest that his views are considered controversial?	6
point out an absurd scenario resulting from an opposing view to his own?	7
mention the unfortunate consequences of taking a positive stance?	8
define prosperity in life in a new way?	9
give an example of well-intentioned ongoing research?	10

CHEER UP: LIFE ONLY GETS BETTER

Humans' capacity for solving problems has been improving our lot for 10,000 years, says Matt Ridley

A The human race has expanded in 10,000 years from less than 10 million people to around 7 billion. Some live in even worse conditions than those in the Stone Age. But the vast majority are much better fed and sheltered, and much more likely to live to old age than their ancestors have ever been. It is likely that by 2110 humanity will be much better off than it is today and so will the ecology of our planet. This view, which I shall call rational optimism, may not be fashionable but it is compelling. This belief holds that the world will pull out of its economic and ecological crises because of the way that markets in goods, services and ideas allow human beings to exchange and specialise for the betterment of all. But a constant drumbeat of pessimism usually drowns out this sort of talk. Indeed, if you dare to say the world is going to go on getting better, you are considered embarrassingly mad.

B Let me make a square concession at the start: the pessimists are right when they say that if the world continues as it is, it will end in disaster. If agriculture continues to depend on irrigation and water stocks are depleted, then starvation will ensue. Notice the word 'if'. The world will not continue as it is. It is my proposition that the human race has become a collective problem-solving machine which solves problems by changing its ways. It does so through invention driven often by the market: scarcity drives up price and that in turn encourages the development of alternatives and efficiencies. History confirms this. When whales grew scarce, for example, petroleum was used instead as a source of oil. The pessimists' mistake is extrapolating: in other words, assuming that the future is just a bigger version of the past. In 1943 IBM's founder Thomas Watson said there was a world market for just five computers – his remarks were true enough at the time, when computers weighed a ton and cost a fortune.

C Many of today's extreme environmentalists insist that the world has reached a 'turning point' – quite unaware that their predecessors have been making the same claim for 200 years. They also maintain that the only sustainable solution is to retreat – to halt economic growth and enter progressive economic recession. This means not just that increasing your company's sales would be a crime, but that the failure to shrink them would be too. But all this takes no account of the magical thing called the collective human brain. There was a time in human history when big-brained people began to exchange things with each other, to become better off as a result. Making and using tools saved time – and the state of being 'better off' is, at the end of the day, simply time saved. Forget dollars or gold. The true measure of something's worth is indeed the hours it takes to acquire it. The more humans diversified as consumers and specialised as producers, and the more they exchanged goods and services, the better off they became. And the good news is there is no inevitable end to this process.

D I am aware that an enormous bubble of debt has burst around the world, with all that entails. But is this the end of growth? Hardly. So long as somebody allocates sufficient capital to innovation, then the credit crunch will not prevent the relentless upward march of human living standards. Even the Great Depression of the 1930s, although an appalling hardship for many, was just a dip in the slope of economic progress. All sorts of new products and industries were born during the depression: by 1937, 40% of Dupont's sales came from products that had barely existed before 1929, such as enamels and cellulose film. Growth will resume – unless it is stifled by the wrong policies. Somebody, somewhere, is still tweaking a piece of software, testing a new material, or transferring a gene that will enable new varieties of rice to be grown in African soils. The latter means some Africans will soon be growing and selling more food, so they will have more money to spend. Some of them may then buy mobile phones from a western company. As a consequence of higher sales, an employee of that western company may get a pay rise, which she may spend on a pair of jeans made from cotton woven in an African factory. And so on. Forget wars, famines and poems. This is history's greatest theme: the metastasis of exchange and specialisation.

Grammar

2   Using the words in brackets and adding any other words you need, turn these notes into sentences that are meaningful and correct.

   EXAMPLE: She / be poor and live in the country / be wealthy and live in a city. (far rather)

   She would far rather be poor and live in the country than be wealthy and live in a city.

   a   He could not have been / with your gift. (thrilled)
   b   Life in retirement / going to work every day. (good deal easy)
   c   There's / glamour in the film business / people like to make out. (not as)
   d   Country life / stimulating / city life. (nowhere)
   e   I / go out on the lake – I / good a swimmer / you are. (sooner not – nothing)
   f   We honestly feel / now / ever before. (fulfilled)
   g   By far / we ever / move to the country. (thing)
   h   She looks / young now / 10 years ago. (as)
   i   Performing on stage /scary / I thought it was going to be. (nothing)
   j   They / walk / go by car. (much sooner)
   k   Looking after a small house / work / looking after a large one. (not as)
   l   Everyone always thinks they / if they / money. (happier)
   m All that good living is making them / ever! (fat)

3 Use the given prompt words to create sentences using the present simple tense. The first one has been done as an example.

EXAMPLE: quicker finish earlier can go
*The **quicker** you **finish**, the **earlier** we **can** all **go** home.*

a bigger   boxer   powerful   punches
....

b heavier   object   faster   fall
....

c warmer   weather   lethargic   become
....

d cleaner   river   fish   find
....

e longer   ferment   better   tastes
....

f longer   read   eyes   hurt
....

Vocabulary

4 Complete these sentences with a noun from the box, using your dictionary to help you. Which are 'happy' and which 'unhappy'?

blues	boots	bump	crest
dumps	heart	moon	spring
tears	weight	whale	world

a We had an absolute .... of a time on holiday.

b There's been a definite .... in his step since he met Joanna.

c He's had the .... ever since he broke up with his girlfriend.

d The sun was shining and she was feeling on top of the ....

e He was over the .... with his new bike.

f She's been a bit down in the .... because she's got to resit her exams.

g Why do arguments with you always reduce me to .... ?

h She was carrying the .... of the world on her shoulders.

i Their hearts were in their .... when they realised they would have to tell him the bad news.

j Realising how little work he had done for his exams brought him down to earth with a ....

k After its election victory, the party was on the .... of a wave.

l His .... leapt when the phone went. Perhaps it would be her?

5 Choose the most appropriate adjective in italics to complete each sentence. Use your dictionary to help you.

a He was very *melancholy / downcast / mournful* when Catherine didn't reply to his letters.

b Don't be too *disheartened / sorrowful / forlorn* – it's only a minor setback.

c The programme shows the *dejected / glum / troubled* mind of a great comedian.

d From across the valley came the *melancholy / miserable / mournful* cry of a wolf.

e The forecast is for more *miserable / downcast / sorrowful* weather at the weekend.

f Going to their rescue in a rowing boat was a bit of a *miserable / forlorn / troubled* hope.

g This is a severely *disturbed / depressed / downcast* economic area.

h When she heard the bad news, she was absolutely *disheartened / inconsolable / glum*.

i It's difficult to smile when your feelings have been *troubled / depressed / hurt*.

j All in all, it's been a pretty *miserable / mournful / forlorn* year for me.

6 The *Cambridge Learner Corpus* shows that candidates often make mistakes with word order in collocations. Correct any mistakes which you see in the following sentences. Some of them are correct.

a Her father worked hard and long to keep the food coming in.

b As soon as she heard the children's voices, she forgot all about her little pains and aches.

c I went there with a group of friends to teach the children how to write and read.

d Moral values, right and wrong, love, confidence and sociability can be learnt at home.

e An important part of every and each learning process is to realise that …

f I think the education I received gave me a sense of good and evil.

g It looked as if he was going to be known wide and far for his music.

h A young person is subject to many strains imposed by the expectations of his dearest and nearest.

i By the law of demand and supply it is inevitable that any economy is in recession.

j The room was full of cobwebs that were difficult to get through because of the bits and pieces left everywhere.

Use of English

7 Read the text below and decide which answer (A, B, C or D) best fits each gap. There is an example at the beginning (0).

Story with a happy ending

A book by a 12-year-old about her own life is (0) ....A.... to be published – 27 years after she wrote it. In the summer of 1979, Clare McCann decided to (1) .... her autobiography. The manuscript (2) .... in a drawer in her house for almost three decades until a decision made on the (3) .... of the moment to send it to a publisher set Clare on a journey that could change her life.

Clare explains, 'It was a project for the school summer holidays and recorded everyday things like family trips, as well as my thoughts on things like music from that era. As I was only 12, I (4) .... the world as shiny and bright and I think that (5) .... in the book. I think kids were (6) .... from the harsh realities of the world a lot more in those days.'

Clare sent the manuscript to an American publishing firm. 'I've now received (7) .... that they want to publish it, and it will be out later this year. I can't wait to see it in (8) ....'

	0	A set	B fixed	C arranged	D established
	1	A scribe	B jot	C pen	D script
	2	A rested	B existed	C hid	D lay
	3	A spur	B cusp	C edge	D spot
	4	A examined	B viewed	C witnessed	D deemed
	5	A points out	B looks over	C turns out	D comes over
	6	A sheltered	B secluded	C shrouded	D screened
	7	A name	B word	C sign	D note
	8	A paper	B type	C print	D copy

18 On freedom

Listening

1 🔊 10 You will hear three different extracts. For questions 1–6, choose the answer (A, B or C) which fits best according to what you hear. There are two questions for each extract.

Extract One

You hear a man and a woman talking about freedom.

1 Both speakers agree that freedom
   A is something not everybody appreciates.
   B can be experienced on different levels.
   C is a term we use far too often.

2 The man got a sense of freedom from
   A facing up to a difficult issue.
   B acting out of concern for others.
   C looking at something in a new way.

Extract Two

You hear a pop singer/songwriter talking about personal freedom in his career.

3 What has the singer realised now that he's older?
   A how useful his course was to him.
   B how disrespectful his attitude was.
   C how pleasant classical music can be.

4 What is the singer critical of?
   A the expectations of the music industry
   B young pop stars' unwillingness to work hard
   C a current trend in musical education

Extract Three

You hear part of an interview about freedom of the press.

5 What is Lucy doing when she talks about the present state of press freedom?
   A criticising the government for trying to limit press freedom
   B justifying the way that journalists obtain their information
   C explaining what she believes her role as a journalist is

6 Lucy mentions the Freedom of Information Act in order to stress
   A the length of time it has taken for the government to become more open.
   B the large number of laws that journalists have to abide by.
   C how it has helped safeguard the privacy of sources.

Vocabulary

2 One word collocates with all the words in the box. Use your dictionary to help you work out what it is, then choose the most appropriate collocation to complete each sentence below. You may need to add a hyphen.

fall	hand	interest	range
scot	set	spirit	standing
time	walk		

a He's been given a .... to negotiate with the kidnappers.

b She was able to .... after the charges against her were dropped.

c All political prisoners are to be .... under the terms of the amnesty.

d As my job isn't too demanding, I am able to do a lot of campaigning in my ....

e The accused got off .... because of lack of evidence.

f I don't mind the extra cost of .... eggs as the hens aren't cooped up in crowded conditions.

g This .... loan from the bank sounds too good to be true!

h The pound appears to be in .... , plunging in value for the fourth successive day.

i Ivy has a highly individual attitude to life – she's a real ....

j The Tokyo Skytree is, at the time of writing, the world's tallest .... tower.

3 Put these words in six groups according to meaning. There are four words in each group. Then decide whether the words in italics in the sentences below are used correctly and, if not, which word(s) from the list would be more appropriate.

autocrat	captive	confinement	
convict	custodian	despot	detention
dictator	elude	escape	evade
flee	free	guard	imprisonment
incarceration	jailbird	keeper	
liberate	prisoner	release	reprieve
tyrant	warder		

EXAMPLE: *autocrat, despot, dictator, tyrant*

a Civil rights groups are demanding the release of the last political *captive*.

b The police have assured the public that the escapees will not *flee* recapture for long.

c He was sentenced to death but the president decided to *liberate* him at the last moment.

d Our mayor sees herself as the *guard* of public morals.

e He claimed that his *detention* for anti-government activities was unlawful.

f He was condemned for being a right-wing *autocrat* who ruled the country by brute force.

4 Complete these sentences with a preposition.

a Animals bred .... captivity would probably not survive .... the wild.

b She was sentenced .... ten years .... California's state penitentiary.

c He's been released .... parole on account of good behaviour.

d Twelve prisoners are .... large following a series of escapes.

e Police are fearful a serial killer might be .... the loose in London.

f He's spent most of his life .... bars.

g She was stopped outside the shop and placed .... arrest.

h The terrorists once again slipped .... the police net.

i She was remanded .... bail until her trial.

j Police are holding the suspect .... custody.

k While she's away, I've got the run .... her house.

Grammar

5 Complete these sentences using an appropriate modal construction with the verbs in brackets. There may be more than one correct answer.

a Up to six books .... (borrow) at a time.

b I .... (phone) if I .... I just didn't get the chance.

c If you hadn't been so lucky, you .... (be injured) more seriously.

d If he had been doing his job properly, he really .... (review) the situation more than once a year.

e If he had entered the competition, he .... (win) a trip to New York.

f Survivors felt there .... (be) an investigation last year into the cause of the disaster.

g You .... (not stay) so late last night to finish the report. You could have done it this morning.

h We were asking for trouble. We really .... (not agree) to go ahead without first finding out what the cost .... (be).

i According to forensic evidence, he .... (not start) the fire.

j I .... (not leave) my keys in the meeting room because I remember having them with me on the way home.

k Judging by her expression, I'd say he .... (tell) her the good news already.

Use of English

6   Read the text below and decide which answer (A, B, C or D) best fits each gap. There is an example at the beginning (0).

Freedom

This morning, the **(0)** ...B... of the villages around Delhi streamed triumphantly towards their rejoicing capital to celebrate the end of a colonization most of them had not even known.

'Oh lovely dawn of freedom that breaks in gold and purple over an ancient capital,' **(1)** .... India's poet laureate in benediction over the crowds. They came from all **(2)** .... There were bullocks, their hoofs painted with orange, green and white stripes, their bells **(3)** .... gaily. There were trucks **(4)** .... with people, their roofs and flanks painted with snakes, eagles and sacred cows. People came on donkey, horse and bicycle, walking and running, country people with turbans of every shape and colour **(5)** .... , the women in bright, festive saris, every bauble they owned **(6)** .... on their arms or faces.

For a **(7)** .... moment rank, religion and caste disappeared. Hindus, Sikhs, Moslems, Anglo-Indians laughed, cheered, and occasionally wept with emotion.
'The British are going,' they cried. 'Nehru is going to **(8)** .... a new flag. We are free!'

0	**A** dwellers	**B** inhabitants	**C** lodgers	**D** inmates
1	**A** proclaimed	**B** stated	**C** testified	**D** indicated
2	**A** edges	**B** positions	**C** sides	**D** views
3	**A** clattering	**B** rattling	**C** jingling	**D** hooting
4	**A** overlapping	**B** overhanging	**C** overriding	**D** overflowing
5	**A** thinkable	**B** imaginable	**C** believable	**D** credible
6	**A** flashing	**B** glaring	**C** scintillating	**D** glittering
7	**A** quick	**B** temporary	**C** transient	**D** brief
8	**A** erect	**B** raise	**C** elevate	**D** lift

7 Read the text below and think of the word which best fits each gap. Use only one word in each gap. There is an example at the beginning (0).

Free of my chains

'Good luck, Frenchman! **(0)** ......From...... this moment you're free. *Adios!*' The officer of the El Dorado penal settlement waved and turned his back. And it was **(1)** .... harder than that for me to free **(2)** .... from the chains I had been dragging behind me these thirteen years. I held Picolino **(3)** .... the arm and we took a few steps up the steep path to the village of El Dorado.

Freedom? Yes, but where? At the far end of the world, as **(4)** .... turned out, way back in the plateaux of Venezuelan Guiana, in a little village deep in the **(5)** .... luxuriant virgin forest you can imagine. This was the south-east tip of Venezuela, close to the Brazilian frontier: an enormous sea of green, broken only here **(6)** .... there by the waterfalls of the rivers that ran through it.

When we had climbed to the edge of the plateau, I breathed in deeply, drawing the air right down into the bottom of my lungs and letting it out gently, **(7)** .... though I were afraid of living these wonderful minutes **(8)** .... fast – these *first minutes of freedom.*

8 Read the text below. Use the word given in capitals at the end of some of the lines to form a word that fits in the gap in the same line. There is an example at the beginning (0).

Free your inner voice

The woman twists and contorts her body, wheeling and spinning
(0) ....spectacularly........ across the room. Her voice rises in   SPECTACLE
(1) .... whoops and yells, then drops to mournful   ECSTASY
moans and grunts before she collapses in a heap on the floor. And then
it's my turn.

I came seeking a brief escape from the stresses of modern life. But right
now my **(2)** .... stress–flight response is in full throttle   INSTINCT
and urging me to sprint for the door, anything rather than stand up and
perform **(3)** .... singing and dancing in front of a rather   SPONTANEITY
forbidding **(4)** .... of complete strangers. But there is no   SORT
(5) .... way out. And something about the trance-like beat   GRACE
of the African drums, the soothing candle-lit glow of the room and the serene
(6) .... of our teacher compels me to stay put.   ASSURE

This is natural voice therapy. The workshops are meant to release hidden
emotions and **(7)** .... and promote relaxation and mental   ANXIOUS
healing. Using a mixture of mantra, Sanskrit chanting, Indian scales and
pure **(8)** .... , the aim is to 'free the inner voice'.   IMPROVISE

Reading

1 You are going to read an article about a TV magician. For questions 1–6, choose the answer (A, B, C or D) which you think fits best according to the text.

Derren Brown, illusionist

Decca Aitkenhead interviews the magician Derren Brown

I wasn't sure what to expect from a book by the illusionist and magician Derren Brown, but it certainly wasn't the great waves of self-loathing that roll out of its pages. *Confessions of a Conjuror* expands into a merciless prosecution of the author's shortcomings – 'my own excruciating personality as a young magician', the occasional 'revolting burst of intellectual smugness', and his 'hateful' failure to sparkle socially in the presence of larger personalities. To this day, he admits that something as simple as mislaying a pen in his 'monstrous London pad' can trigger a whole new wave of fury.

The author doesn't sound at all like the coolly omnipotent, slightly cocky character we have grown used to from TV. For well over a decade now, Brown has been entertaining audiences with a blend of hypnotism, magic, illusion, mind games and elaborately ambitious stunts. In 2003 he memorably appeared to play Russian Roulette on live TV, and

21 more recently caused even more consternation by appearing to guess the winning lottery numbers.

23 Critics call him a fraud – an old-fashioned illusionist masquerading as a master of psychology,

25 who passes off trickery as mind reading – but the televised stunts attract viewers in their millions, while his live stage shows sell out nationwide to

28 fans thrilled by the audacity of his intrigue.

So I wonder which Brown I'm about to meet when I arrive at his London apartment. The answer, it turns out, is neither. The man who opens the door doesn't even look like Derren Brown. He is much more casually scruffy and unremarkable than his stage persona – less theatrical, less pointy-looking – with the innocuous sort of face that blends effortlessly into crowds. He seems like someone light-footed and comfortable, quick to laugh and instantly likeable, to all appearances blithely untroubled by anything. 'I don't play up to that guy off the TV,' he readily agrees, 'because I wouldn't particularly want to meet him in the flesh. That rather controlling sort of thing – I don't think that's a nice way of being with people, so I never for a second want to be that person. I think it's important to be sort of nice.' He's not very nice about himself, though, I say – not in his book, anyway. To my surprise, he looks taken aback when I point out this contradiction.

'Really? Oh. That must just be my tone. In terms of self-esteem and confidence I think I'm generally quite healthy.' The book, he ponders – which is not so much an autobiography as a 'semi-autobiographical whimsy' – is loosely structured around a time in the 90s when he worked as a performing magician in a restaurant. 'You're going up to a group of people at the table who are happily eating, and going "I'm the magician!". I mean, you couldn't sound like more of an irritation. And you've got to do it 50 times a night. So maybe the book is rooted in that feeling.'

His flat is sensationally weird – part gentleman's club, part museum, every room a freaky spectacle crammed with taxidermy and esoterica. Surrounded by all his stuffed giraffes and snakes' skeletons, Brown looks hilariously incongruous. He talks easily and unselfconsciously, is never defensive but always relaxed and engaged. Yet no matter how hard I try, I can't get him to say why he does what he does, or what he loves about it. 'It's just sort of what I'm doing, I suppose,' he offers vaguely.

Only three people know how he does his stunts; Channel 4, he grins, 'have no idea', not even about his infamous Russian Roulette stunt. 'At the end of the day it was a piece of live entertainment and I knew what I was doing,' is all he will say. 'But you know, the reality is that I don't like saying how it was done, any more than saying how anything else is done. If I was utterly honest about everything then it wouldn't be very entertaining. Part of what keeps it fresh and interesting to me is finding new ways to have your cake and eat it at times.'

I feel none the wiser, but the really odd thing is that in all the time I am with him, not one of his answers seems less than satisfactory. Something about his voice is extraordinarily persuasive, and in his presence his whole manner is so beguilingly lovely that it's not until I listen to the tape afterwards that I realise, to my surprise, how often he sidesteps a question, while never giving the impression of being evasive. I still have no idea if he's really riddled with self-contempt, or secretly rather pleased with himself. And yet he had seemed like the most forthcoming of interviewees.

1 What does Brown say in his book is one thing that he dislikes about himself?
   A his forgetfulness
   B his smallness
   C his shyness
   D his rashness

2 Which phrase refers to what his critics see as Brown making false claims?
   A caused even more consternation (line 21)
   B an old-fashioned illusionist (lines 23–24)
   C passes off trickery (line 25)
   D the audacity of his intrigue (line 28)

3 In the third paragraph, Brown confirms what the writer is thinking about
   A his neurotic personality.
   B his mastery of the art of disguise.
   C him needing to be in control of situations.
   D him having a separate identity in real life.

4 What is Brown's explanation for the apparent contradiction the writer picks up on?
   A His book looks back to a time in his life which wasn't very enjoyable.
   B He has to be careful about what he divulges in public.
   C He finds it surprisingly hard to verbalise his feelings.
   D His book was designed to dispel a myth.

5 What idea is present in both the fifth and sixth paragraphs?
   A that Brown is in fact highly ambitious
   B that Brown says one thing and means another
   C that Brown is intent on cultivating his own image
   D that Brown does not like to reveal much information

6 The writer implies that the whole interview
   A has been rather a waste of time.
   B has left her feeling distinctly uneasy.
   C has made her realise something about herself.
   D has been like one of Brown's conjuring tricks.

Vocabulary

2 Complete each sentence with one of the onomatopoeic verbs from the box in the correct form.

beep	bubble	chatter	clap	crunch
flutter	giggle	hiccup	hum	mumble
plop	rustle	slurp	thud	

a It was so cold outside my teeth started ....

b It was spooky in there, and I .... a tune to myself to try and stay calm.

c The bird flew so close to me I could hear its wings ....

d When the microwave .... , it's time to take the dish out.

e I'll never forget the sound of his head .... against the wall.

f The audience .... in appreciation of the comedian's performance.

g The boy dropped the stone from the bridge and it .... into the water below.

h He gulped down his food too fast and then .... for several minutes.

i I know he's a bit shy, but he's got to learn to speak up and stop ....

j When the soup came to the boil, we could hear it ....

k I love the sound of the snow .... under my walking boots.

l Some teenage girls were .... over the photos they'd taken of each other.

m Don't .... your soup – it's bad manners!

n I could hear the wonderful sound of the leaves .... in the wind.

3 Complete each sentence by forming a new word from the word in capital letters.

a He claimed to have seen a strange .... at night. APPEAR

b The film is all about the dark and .... side of the human condition. DESTROY

c The doctor dismissed my fears as totally .... LOGIC

d From my hotel window I could hear the .... sound of the waves breaking on the shore. HYPNOSIS

e 'The play was absolutely dire, ... bad,' said Ruby. BELIEVE

f We proceeded .... into the haunted bedroom. EASY

g The researchers were investigating the .... side of the human brain. INSTINCT

h I'm sure any resemblance between them is merely .... COINCIDENCE

i Don't worry; there is absolutely no .... evidence for this claim. SCIENCE

j To date, nobody has been able to come up with an .... EXPLAIN

k I just cannot work out how he pulled off that magical trick – it's just .... COMPREHEND

Grammar

4 Identify the incorrectly or inappropriately positioned adverbs / adverbial phrases in these sentences and reposition them. There may be more than one correct answer.

EXAMPLE: Unfortunately, the witnesses by the time we got there already had in panic fled the building and there no longer was any sign of a ghost.

Unfortunately, the witnesses had already fled the building in panic by the time we got there and there was no longer any sign of a ghost.

a Alone he sits all day long in his room, writing painstakingly up by hand his findings, on mostly scrap paper and usually in unfathomably long and complex sentences.

b The fortune-teller's predictions to my astonishment turned out to be accurate uncannily.

c Strangely enough, although it was dark practically, I was feeling actually relaxed quite as I patiently waited for a glimpse of the apparition, but that naturally dramatically changed when the room all of a sudden went cold.

d Never I've seen anything quite look so eerie or move so strangely – out of my wits I was terrified!

e There hadn't curiously been any further sightings of the ghost in the castle since last summer the previous owner left.

f The other day for the carnival he was very made up realistically – he just looked like the ghost of an old woman.

g Always he speaks on the subject of the paranormal intelligently, but the talk he later was giving generally was expected to be better even than usual.

h The computer for some reason started behaving rather oddly in the back office, flashing inexplicably up onto the screen strangely disturbing messages.

Use of English

5 Complete the second sentence so that it has a similar meaning to the first sentence, using the word given. Do not change the word given. You must use between three and eight words, including the word given.

1 It seemed there was nothing the magician couldn't do.

limits

It seemed there ....
.... capabilities.

2 With things like the existence of ghosts, I think we should remain open-minded.

open

I think it's important to keep ....
.... comes to things like ghosts.

3 I found the incident in that room really frightening.

went

What..
a fright.

4 I'm extremely dubious about the existence of ghosts.

doubt

I very ....
thing as a ghost.

5 The socialist party candidate is easily winning the election campaign.

representing

The woman ....
.... away with the election campaign.

6 There's still a faint possibility that the deal can be finalised by tomorrow's deadline.

glimmer

There's still a ....
.... time for tomorrow's deadline.

Listening

1 🔊 **11** You are going to hear a talk from a woman called Emma Coleman about university student pranks, or practical jokes. For questions 1–9, complete the sentences with a word or short phrase.

In Cambridge in 1958 a student prank gave the illusion that a car was moving against the **(1)** ....

The pranksters pretended the car was publicising a **(2)** .... so as to avoid suspicion.

Some of the pranksters used **(3)** .... to create a bridge which the lifting group could walk on.

Fortunately for the prank, some suspicious policemen were distracted by **(4)** .... who were passing the scene.

Some student sportspeople were persuaded that the object dangling in the sky was a **(5)** .... that had been attached there.

The car was eventually dismantled by workmen using **(6)** ....

The secret of how the prank was done was revealed, to the disappointment of **(7)** .... , in 2008.

The leader of the pranksters, Peter Davey, later became an expert in the field of **(8)** ....

The speaker, Emma Coleman, stresses that her interest is in student pranks that give no **(9)** .... to the intended victim.

Grammar

2 Complete these sentences using an appropriate form of *have* or *get* with an appropriate form of the verb in brackets. There may be more than one correct answer.

EXAMPLE: I won't be long. I'm just going to *get* my hair *cut*. (cut)

a Haven't you .... the sound system .... yet? (set up)

b When are you next .... the stage curtains .... ? (clean)

c She .... her unicycle .... last week. (steal)

d Can you .... someone .... the costumes to the studio for me? (deliver)

e I .... a very strange thing .... to me on my way home last night. (happen)

f He .... himself .... with a hilarious costume from the wardrobe department. (kit out)

g It's wonderful to .... people .... themselves in the old theatre again. (enjoy)

h She insisted on .... the theatre .... by a feng shui expert. (analyse)

i .... everyone .... outside the audition room till their name is called. (wait)

j The comedian soon .... us .... our heads off. (laugh)

k I won't .... you .... your weight around in here. (throw)

l I won't .... my auditorium .... a circus. (turn into)

m Why don't you .... Nicole .... to the party? (come)

n The administrator .... everybody .... application forms. (fill out)

o If you don't leave immediately, I'll .... you .... (arrest)

p Unfortunately we didn't .... the star of the show. (meet)

q He .... his foot .... in the curtains as they were closing. (catch)

r After you have .... the costumes .... , can you tidy up the props? (finish)

s Whatever you do, don't .... them .... jokes. (tell)

t Once we .... the lights .... , the studio warmed up really quickly. (work)

Vocabulary

3 Which of the words in the box below ...

a are synonyms for *amusing*?

b are synonyms for *smile*?

c are synonyms for *laugh*?

d are both verbs and nouns?

e are adjectives that can apply to people?

f involve making a sound?

g carry negative implications?

beam	cackle	chuckle	droll
facetious	giggle	grin	humorous
hysterical	jocular	roar	smirk
snigger	snort	titter	

4 Complete these sentences using the correct form of *go* or *stop* with the words in the box and an article if necessary. There may be more than one correct answer.

at (× 2)	by (× 2)	down	in	for
into	of	off (× 2)	over (× 2)	
to (× 2)	up (× 2)			

EXAMPLE: I was passing your house, so I thought I'd *stop by* for a coffee.

a She's really making .... her new career.

b I'm sorry, madam, but we have to .... the rules.

c The car slowed down and gradually came ....

d I'll .... at the shops on my way home and get some bread.

e I'd rather not .... that now. Can we discuss it later?

f There's a gas leak and the whole building could .... at any time.

g He's one of those people who will .... nothing to achieve his goals.

h I've .... the mouse hole with newspaper for now.

i Your speech would have .... better if you'd left out those appalling jokes.

j Have you ever thought of .... medicine as a career?

k He used to smoke in bed when I first got to know him – I soon put .... that!

l Will you have .... opening this jar for me? I can't do it.

m The alarm should .... automatically as soon as smoke is detected.

n I've .... these lines time and again but I still keep forgetting them.

o They're .... in Malaysia for a couple of nights on the way to Australia.

5 Complete these tips with words from the box and underline the point of humour in each sentence, where the writer does not follow his or her own advice.

~~agree~~	always	apostrophe	avoid
clichés	commas	contractions	
correctly	diminutive	double	end
exclamation	fragments	generalise	
proofread	puns	specific	split
start	unnecessary		

EXAMPLE: Verbs <u>has</u> to *agree* with their subjects.

a Prepositions are not words to .... sentences with.

b And don't .... a sentence with a conjunction.

c It is wrong to ever .... an infinitive.

d Avoid .... like the plague.

e Also, ... avoid annoying alliteration.

f Be more or less ....

g Parenthetical remarks (however relevant) are (usually) ....

h No sentence ....

i .... aren't necessary and shouldn't be used.

j One should never ....

k Don't use no .... negatives.

l .... ampersands & abbreviations, etc.

m Eliminate .... , that are, not necessary.

n Never use a big word when a .... one would suffice.

o Kill all .... marks!!!

p Use words .... , irregardless of how others use them.

q Use the .... in it's proper place and omit it when its not needed.

r .... are for children, not groan readers.

s .... carefully to see if you any words out.

6 The *Cambridge Learner Corpus* shows that candidates often make mistakes with prepositions. Correct these mistakes made by Proficiency candidates.

    a Nowadays we live differently than years ago.

    b Don't get depressed. Try to look always for the bright side.

    c Considering the importance of this visit and also taking in account who he was …

    d I would like to express my dissatisfaction on reference to the TV I bought from your store.

    e Sometimes they would permit me, under my own risk, to …

    f If they were all calm in nature, the experience would be positive for them.

    g It may help to give you a new perspective about things.

    h People behaved in a rude way, shouting and shoving with no reason.

    i The Eastern Culture course is with high demand.

Use of English

7 Complete the second sentence so that it has a similar meaning to the first sentence using the word given. Do not change the word given. You must use between three and eight words including the word given.

    1 Although she was upset, there was never any question of revenge.

      last

      Upset as ....

      on her mind.

    2 They pulled out all the stops for their daughter's wedding.

      nothing

      As far as their ....

      much for them.

    3 It is a good idea for parents to overlook their children's minor misdemeanours.

      blind

      As a parent, it helps if ....

      your children's minor misdemeanours.

    4 She hasn't stopped for a break in the five hours she's been here.

      go

      She's .... five hours ago.

    5 I very nearly told her what I thought, but in the end decided not to.

      short

      In the end, I .... feelings.

    6 Somebody broke into her car last week.

      broken

      She .... last week.

Writing workout 1

Letter

1 Complete this advice on writing a 'letter to the editor' by matching the two halves of the sentences.

1	Open clearly	**a**	engage the reader.
2	End on a	**b**	range of vocabulary.
3	Be sure to	**c**	paragraphing.
4	Develop the topic in	**d**	are accurate.
5	Include a good balance	**e**	with a reason for writing.
6	Use appropriate register	**f**	illustrating or reinforcing points you're making.
7	Demonstrate a wide		
8	Use anecdote or example as a means of	**g**	of comment and opinion.
		h	and format.
9	Order points	**i**	strong note.
10	Use effective	**j**	logically and coherently.
11	Make sure grammar and spelling	**k**	a relevant way.

2 Read this extract from a magazine article on play behaviour among animals.

The end seemed very near for Hudson, a Canadian Eskimo dog tethered near the shore of Hudson Bay east of Churchill, Manitoba. A 1,000 lb polar bear was lumbering toward the dog and about 40 others, the prized possessions of Brian Ladoon, a hunter and trapper. It was mid-November; ice had not yet formed on the bay, and the open water prevented bears from hunting their favourite prey, seals. So this bear had been virtually fasting for four months. Surely a dog was destined to become a meal.

The bear closed in. Did Hudson howl in terror and try to flee? On the contrary. He wagged his tail, grinned, and actually bowed to the bear, as if in invitation. The bear responded with enthusiastic body language and nonaggressive facial signals. These two normally antagonistic species were speaking the same language: 'Let's play!'

The romp was on. For several minutes dog and bear wrestled and cavorted. Once the bear completely wrapped himself around the dog like a friendly white cloud. Bear and dog then embraced, as if in sheer abandon.

Every evening for more than a week the bear returned to play with one of the dogs. Finally the ice formed, and he set off for his winter habitat.

This behaviour has been witnessed repeatedly in Churchill but has not been reported elsewhere in the Arctic. Throughout the region, polar bears occasionally kill and eat sled dogs.

3 If you wanted to respond by writing a 'letter to the editor', expressing your views on play and play behaviour, how might you order the following paragraph plan?

a establish a starting point for discussion through personal opinion

b introduce the subject of the letter / reason for writing

c extend the discussion in a new direction

d develop the discussion with reference to the article and personal experience

e conclude by questioning the implications for modern society

4 **Correct the spelling mistakes in this paragraph.**

I tend to think of play as spontanious behaviour that has no clear-cut goal and does not conform to a stereotipical pattern, and your article would seem to encourage such a view. To me the purpose of play is simply play itself; it appears to be pleasureable. But play also has benefits: it is key to an individuals development, social relationship's and status.

5 **Complete this paragraph with linkers from the box.**

as (× 2)	but also	furthermore	in my view
namely	not only	while	

(1) .... a dog-owner, I know play is vital for proper development in dogs: games of keep away, chase and tug-of-war (2) .... develop physical abilities (3) .... help the animals attain social status by establishing superior mental and physical skills. (4) .... , play, (5) .... it often mimics aggression, (6) .... in the article, is one form of defence used to defuse potential confrontations. (7) .... , ritualised play in humans, (8) .... sports, serves an identical purpose.

6 **Choose the best alternative in italics to complete this paragraph.**

[1]*Recent / Up-to-date* research [2]*says / suggests* that play may be as important for us and other [3]*animals / creations* as sleeping and dreaming. And no-one would [4]*argue / dispute* that play is an important part of a [5]*healthy / well,* happy childhood. But if play is necessary for the [6]*active / physical* and [7]*sociable / social* development of young animals, [8]*including / namely* humans, what [9]*happens / occurs* if young creatures are [10]*hampered / prevented* from playing or [11]*exploited / maltreated* with the result that their play is [12]*abnormal / unusual*? Their [13]*development / growth* may also be abnormal. [14]*Certainly / Surely* the [15]*behaviour / tricks* of 'problem dogs' [16]*invariably / regularly* develops through [17]*improper / indecent* games or lack of games when they were young.

7 **Match the paragraphs in exercises 4–6 to an appropriate section of the paragraph plan in exercise 3 and order them accordingly. Then add an appropriate salutation, introduction and final paragraph to arrive at a complete 'letter to the editor'.**

Writing workout 2

Review

1 Which of these should a good review include? Tick the boxes which apply.

a mix of information and opinion ☐
b full details of what is being reviewed ☐
c name/title of what is being reviewed ☐
d mix of negative and positive points ☐
e relevant comparisons ☐
f examples to illustrate points ☐
g evaluation and recommendation ☐
h range of vocabulary, including specialist terms ☐
i variety of linkers and grammatical structures ☐
j personal anecdotes and hearsay ☐

2 Is either of these texts a review? Why? / Why not?

A

Born in 1930 in East London, Harold Pinter began to publish poetry in periodicals before he was twenty, then became a professional actor, working mainly in repertory. His first play, *The Room*, was performed in Bristol in 1957, followed in 1958 by a London production of *The Birthday Party*. Pinter's distinctive voice was soon recognized, and many critical and commercial successes followed, including *The Caretaker* (1960) and *No Man's Land* (1975).

Pinter's gift for portraying, by means of dialogue which realistically produces nuances of colloquial speech, the difficulties of communication and the many layers of meaning in language, pause, and silence, has created a style labelled by the popular imagination as 'Pinteresque', and his themes – nameless menace, erotic fantasy, obsession and jealousy, family hatreds and mental disturbance – are equally recognizable.

B

Harold Pinter's plays invite interpretation and reject it at the same time. You wouldn't be human if you didn't want to know what they mean, what is actually going on in them. But you soon learn that there can be no neat answers to such questions. The formula that will reveal all is beyond one's grasp.

No Man's Land, which has been revived at London's Lyttleton Theatre, is particularly tantalising in this respect. You never do learn the truth about the pasts of the two elderly men – one prosperous, one down-at-heel – who, attended by two possibly threatening subordinates, compulsively reminisce. They may be old friends; more probably, one has inveigled his way into the memories of the other, just as he has sidled into his house. What makes the impact is the galvanising self-descriptions. It's as if the dialogue has its own life – as if the characters become airborne on stories, talking their way into existence, out of the no man's land that is old age.

Optional writing task

With reference to exercise 2, and incorporating your own ideas, write a 280–320 word review of a well-known play or musical you have seen, focusing in particular on the interplay of themes and characterisation. Or, if you prefer, continue with exercises 3–7.

3 Choose the best alternative in italics to complete this review introduction.

On the page, Harold Pinter's *No Man's Land* is enough to give the reader a panic attack. The literary ¹*allusions / mentions* are so ²*dense / thick*, the dislocation of character so mysterious that pinning down what's going on is ³*as hard as anything / like chasing a drop of water through a fountain*. But it's striking how little this matters in performance. ⁴*Directed / Managed* by the ⁵*screenwriter / playwright*, at London's Lyttleton Theatre, this most metaphysical of Pinter's plays is immediate, fully fleshed and ⁶*filled / packed* with social detail.

4 Put the adjectives in the box into the text below. Ignore the asterisks for now.

hidden	imposing	inner	seedy
seeming	shabby	sharp	

The two central characters are (1) .... opposites. They are* bound together by a (2) .... affinity. Hirst is a successful literary man. *He lives in a really (3) .... house in Hampstead. Hirst invites Spooner home*. Spooner is a (4) .... pub worker from Chalk Farm. Hirst's life represents everything that Spooner has dreamed of. For Hirst, Spooner stands for what he might have become. *It's not just about success and failure. Hirst's success has turned to ashes. He is a heavy drinker, living in a state of moral paralysis. But it is only outwardly that Spooner embodies what he has escaped from. The (5) .... guest is also an emanation of the well-dressed host's (6) .... emptiness. There is a sense of tragic waste in the play, of things left undone. *There is some (7) .... and perceptive comedy. This new production does equal justice to both aspects.

5 At present the sentences in the paragraph in exercise 4 are rather short and disjointed. Improve the style of the paragraph in the places indicated with an asterisk (*). This might involve using a linker or relative pronoun.

6 Put the letters of the words in brackets in the right order to complete this paragraph. The first and last letters are given.

The leads are (1) t...................c (trfieirc). Corin Redgrave as Hirst and John Wood as Spooner both give (2) s...................e (slaupvierte) performances. Wood, on the surface all genial and (3) h...................s (hmsealrs), also comes over as disturbingly (4) c...................g (cninung) and manipulative, while Redgrave's (5) f...................y (ftsory) arrogance is brilliantly done. Though Danny Dyer is (6) u...................g (uisnnirpnig) as one manservant, Andy de la Tour has the (7) i...................g (irtinatagnig) manner of the other servant down to perfection.

7 Combine your paragraphs from exercises 3–6, adding paragraph breaks as appropriate, to arrive at a complete review.

Writing workout 3

Essay

1 Choose the option (a or b) which you think best applies to an essay.

1 **a** factual   **b** discursive
2 **a** continuous prose   **b** sections and sub-sections
3 **a** fiction   **b** non-fiction
4 **a** a specific topic   **b** no specific topic
5 **a** informal   **b** neutral

2 Note down some ideas for and against spending money on exploring space. Try to think of two reasons why it is worth spending money on and two reasons why it is not a good idea. Here are some words and phrases that might help you.

> world population   scientific discoveries
> natural resources   political problems
> hunger   economic crisis

3 Read these two short texts about space exploration. Underline the two key points in each text and compare them with your notes for exercise 2.

Into space

When Armstrong set foot on the moon, it was a triumph for the engineers and scientists who made it possible. The innovations they were responsible for were immensely beneficial to us all because they could be applied to other fields, although this is not widely recognised. The stark reality is that it is very much in our long-term interest to take space exploration seriously. The most pessimistic forecasts envisage a global population of 16 billion by 2100. To make matters worse, the world's resources are dwindling rapidly. Space exploration is a first step towards colonising new worlds and potentially solving both problems.

Back to Earth

We should never forget that space exploration was originally driven first and foremost by political ambitions and rivalries. This remains the case. Any country wishing to demonstrate its power on the global stage will sooner or later send astronauts into space. We now hear that NASA is demanding a budget of $19 billion. My question is just how many hospitals and schools could this fund? Space exploration is a colossal waste of money, particularly when famine and disease remain the fate of millions. With such problems staring us in the face, it seems that our priorities are wrong.

4 Here are some more ideas about space exploration. Which of these ideas are linked to the four points you identified in exercise 3 and which ideas are *completely new*? Write *N* for new ideas not covered in the original texts.

1 Launching a rocket is hardly the most environmentally-friendly action. Think of the millions of tons of rocket fuel that are required.

2 Some scientists believe that the asteroid belt between Mars and Jupiter could be a rich source of precious metals and minerals.

3 The so-called "space race" of the 1950s and 1960s did not benefit the world at all. In fact, it only led to the production of ever more sophisticated military technology.

4 It is important for us to get some perspective on human affairs, and often the only way we can do that is to see the Earth from space. We need to be reminded that the Earth is just an insignificant speck in the vastness of space, and that the things we incessantly worry about are really not very important at all.

5 Many areas of human life have indirectly benefited from the work of NASA and other space agencies. Breakthroughs that were originally made as part of the space programme have also been useful for surgeons conducting complicated operations, builders constructing offices and homes, and the manufacturers of both cars and planes.

6 Surely the most fundamental question that needs addressing is exactly how life developed on our planet and whether conditions exist elsewhere in the universe for other life forms.

7 If countries spent even a fraction of the money they spend on the development of space rockets and probes to solving the serious problems of famine and mass starvation, then the world would be a much better place.

8 It may be unwise to pour money into programmes that aim to pick up signals from other planets and to make contact with aliens. We cannot be sure that any alien civilisation to which we extended the hand of friendship would be benevolent in its intentions.

5 You have been asked to respond to the points in the texts and to evaluate them. You can either support the points or disagree with them. Decide if these student responses support the key points in the two texts or disagree with them. Write *S* for 'support' and *D* for 'disagree'.

A Evangelists for space exploration push the idea of colonising distant worlds, and their enthusiasm is admirable. The implausibility of this vision should trouble anyone who thinks for a moment about it. The moon and Mars are inhospitable, barren worlds. We would never even be able to set foot on the surface without a spacesuit. And as for the nearest planets outside the solar system, they are hundreds of years away.

B It is easy for the cynics to go back into the history books and remind us that the race to put a man on the moon was tinged with political motivations. This is a fair point but it overlooks what has happened since. We now have an international space station which brings former rivals together in a spirit of co-operation.

C Within 50 years reserves of metals such as zinc, gold, silver, tin and copper could be exhausted. These are vital to our manufacturing industries and there are no obvious replacements lined up. Despite the cost of mining such metals on the surface of neighbouring planets and asteroids, it may be the only option open to us.

D It can be argued that turning our backs on the space programme shows a lack of vision and imagination. Yet lacking compassion is a greater failing in my judgement. Estimates of nearly 900 million people without enough to eat on a daily basis should be enough to make even the biggest advocates of the space programme think again.

6 In a discursive essay you can take a strong position for or against an idea. However, it is a good idea to show some awareness that there is another side to the argument. Look again at the four extracts in exercise 5 and identify the sentences which show the writer is aware there is another side to the argument.

Optional writing task

Write an essay summarising the key points in the two texts in exercise 3 and giving your opinion on them. You should include your own ideas. You can also use the ideas from exercises 4 and 5 if you wish. Make sure your style and tone are appropriate for an essay and that you use a range of appropriate vocabulary. You should also make sure your answer is well organised, with a variety of linking words and phrases. Your answer should be about 240–280 words.

7 Which of these sentences do you think would be best to introduce an essay on space exploration containing the four points you identified in exercise 3? Give reasons for your answers.

a I remember my parents telling me about Neil Armstrong landing on the moon and how thrilled they were. My father was only a boy but he was so excited he could hardly sleep.

b Space exploration has some big advantages. On the other hand, there are some obvious disadvantages too.

c Since the dawn of time human beings have always sought to explore and to extend their knowledge of the world around them. Space exploration is the latest expression of this basic human instinct, yet the expenditure of vast sums of money on it remains highly controversial.

d It is ridiculous to claim that we have benefited from the space programme. Many of the innovations space scientists say they are responsible for would have happened anyway, even if NASA and other space agencies had never existed.

8 The final paragraph of an essay is very important. It is an opportunity to leave the reader with a positive final impression and bring the essay to a satisfying conclusion. Which of these things (a–c) do you think would be the best way to conclude the essay on space exploration if you were writing about 240–280 words?

a A summary of the points you have already made earlier in the essay.

b A strong re-statement of your opinion for or against, possibly supported by some new information.

c A statement that says this topic is controversial and it is difficult to have a clear opinion for or against.

Writing workout 4

Article

1 In any article, which of these are important for holding a reader's attention and which are important for attracting it in the first place? Write H (holding), A (attracting) or B (both).

1 appropriate style and tone ☐
2 appropriate register for target readers ☐
3 a variety of grammatical structures and stylistic devices ☐
4 a good range of vocabulary and expressions ☐
5 a catchy title ☐
6 an interesting angle ☐
7 an intriguing opening paragraph ☐
8 clear development of subject/topic ☐
9 a strong final message ☐
10 a logical structure and smooth flow ☐

2 Compare the two photos below and choose a word or phrase from each pair (1–6) to describe each photo.

The Motorbike – Honda CBR 1000rr Fireblade, icon of modern motorcycling

The Scooter – Honda FES250 Foresight, the last of its kind and still the best!

1 adventure / commuting
2 convenience / power
3 impression of glamour / impression of reliability
4 economy / performance
5 practicality / thrills
6 built for comfort / built for style

3 Complete this paragraph with words from the box.

capacity	combination
features	handling
models	performance

A pleasing **(1)** .... of surprisingly sleek aerodynamic styling, smooth **(2)** .... and spacious carrying **(3)** .... , the Honda Foresight is quite simply a legend. It delivers near motorcycle-level **(4)** .... with confident control at all times, making it an effective low-grade cruiser as well as an excellent commuter.
(5) .... include Honda's Dual Combined Braking system, used on Honda's larger **(6)** ....

Optional writing task

A college magazine editor has invited contributions to a special feature entitled 'Getting around: motorbike or scooter?' With reference to exercises 1–3 and incorporating your own ideas, write a 280–320 word article for the feature. Or, if you prefer, continue with exercises 4–9.

4 Compare these three paragraphs as possible openers for the article in the writing task. Which do you think is most appropriate and why? Think about angle, style and tone.

> **A** People who ride powerful motorcycles tend to look down on scooters because they don't conform to their lifestyle image. However scooters make up an important part of the two-wheeled market and offer a great deal more than the economy and convenience for which they have a reputation.

> **B** Mention motorbikes and most people think of speed, excitement, glamour, adventure and the freedom of the open road. Mention scooters, on the other hand, and more mundane considerations like economy, comfort, convenience, practicality and reliability probably come to mind. Yet scooters come in all shapes and sizes. Are they really all bought by sad individuals who can't hack a real bike? If that's what you think, read on and prepare to be surprised.

> **C** Scooters are so cool. I've had mine for three weeks now and love it to bits. I couldn't imagine life without it. It's blue and I call it 'Scoot'. It's got so much going for it – it's cheap to run, ever so convenient, incredibly easy to ride and wonderfully trendy. Everybody wants a scooter these days – have you noticed how many more there are on the road? I don't know much about motorcycles, but what do I need to know? As far as I'm concerned, scooters are where it's at.

5 Complete the next paragraph with words from the box. Which paragraph in exercise 4 is it closest to in style?

all	along with	already	but
just	still	to date	when

> At (1) .... over ten years old, the machine I own has (2) .... clocked up some 150,000 km and is (3) .... running. It was purchased for travel, not for showing off or racing between motorway stops, (4) .... for covering long distances economically, conveniently and comfortably. (5) .... , I have covered 34 different countries on various trips, (6) .... using the bike for the more usual transportation at home – (7) .... on incredibly low fuel consumption, and sustaining 120 kph (8) .... travelling along on roads.

6 Find words in the paragraph in exercise 5 which you can replace with these more colourful collocations to make the paragraph more interesting.

a adventure expeditions
b convenient commuting
c going strong
d cruising steadily
e service areas
f two-wheeler

7 Use the words in the box to make three collocations which you can use to complete the paragraph below. Then rewrite the opening sentence as a rhetorical question that links appropriately to the paragraph in exercise 5.

aerodynamic	luggage	bodywork
seat	compartment	padded

> The source of such a wonderful mix of convenience, economy and adventure is a Honda, but not a new Fireblade – a humble Foresight. Yes, 250cc of value for money and dependability, its .... is still state-of-the-art, with a comfortable .... and a handy .... It won't pull wheelies, but it will hold a steady 120 kph and comfortably cover 700+ kilometres without refuelling.

8 Which of these points might you consider including in the final paragraph of the article? Tick the boxes that apply and write a final paragraph.

☐ a list of places the writer has travelled to and what he found there
☐ an evaluation of the Foresight's performance against the writer's purchase criteria
☐ a description of how well the Foresight has worn
☐ details of any concerns the writer might have

9 Choose a title for the article from the list.

a Travelling with Foresight …
b My two-wheeler and I
c Why I like my scooter

Writing workout 5

Report

1 Complete the sentences with words from the box.

> bullets and signposting   a brief introduction   content plan
> grammatical structures   neutral tone   the point
> purpose   the target reader   the target reader

How to write a good report

a Start with a clear picture of the scope and the .... of the report.

b Keep .... in mind at all times and aim to inform.

c Draw up a detailed .... organised around a clear structure.

d Start with .... that links with the title.

e Use effective paragraphing and other organising devices such as

.... , as appropriate.

f Use an impersonal style and .... throughout.

g Use a good range of relevant vocabulary and a variety of ....

h Be succinct and keep to ....

i Use a level of formality that is appropriate to ....

2 Look at this extract from a course brochure. Who is the course for and what is DTP?

GOOD DESIGN USING DTP

Duration:	2 days
Venue:	The Training Centre, Regent Street, London
Tutor:	Will Render

They gave you a desktop-publishing system and now they expect you to design ads, brochures, leaflets and reports, but you're not a trained designer. Don't worry – practical help is at hand! After this comprehensive and highly enjoyable two-day course you'll be producing work to be proud of.

Programme:

Design considerations with DTP	*What software to use*
Typography and fonts	*Font size and style*
Layout and balance	*Designing on-screen*
Graphics and logos	*Looking for the original angle*
Colour considerations	*Making the most of colour*
Proofing and printing	*Colour proofs / film output*
Practical exercises	*Hands-on experience*

Optional writing task

Imagine you were sent on *Good Design using DTP* by the company you work for. With reference to exercises 1 and 2 and incorporating your own ideas, write a 280–320 word report on the course for your boss. Make up any information you need. Or, if you prefer, continue with exercises 3–7.

3 What do you think of this as an introduction to a report? How would you change it to make it more suitable?

> My reason for writing is because I attended the course *Good Design using DTP*. Let me begin with general arrangements. I'll then go on to course content and finally I'll conclude with my evaluation and recommendation.

4 Without omitting any information, reduce this passage to about 120 words by deleting redundant words and phrases and by substituting more 'economical' words and structures where possible. Add any paragraph breaks you think are necessary.

> The *Good Design using DTP* course took place at the programmed venue of The Training Centre, an impressive building situated in the heart of London's Regent Street, on January 13–14. The facilities at The Training Centre premises could only be described as excellent. For a start, the computing room was large and spacious, a really good size, and it was also extremely well equipped and altogether very comfortable; each participant was assigned his or her own dedicated computer terminal to work on for the duration of the whole course, which was obviously ideal for getting a maximum of hands-on experience. The course was attended by a total of seven participants altogether. All seven participants had already had some experience of – but no training in – DTP. In essence this added up to a homogeneous group of beginners with compatible interests and abilities. The arrangements that were in place throughout the course were faultless and timings were consistently punctual. It was also heart-warming to find that there was a really good supply of refreshments on hand during the day and discover that considerable trouble had been taken with the lunches, which were very enjoyable. (193 words)

5 There are three errors of content in the following paragraph. Check back against the course details in exercise 2 to find and correct them, then rewrite the paragraph in a format that is clearer and uses fewer words.

> The three-day programme was quite intensive, covering a range of DTP functions and features. These were design software considerations with DTP, including what hardware to use, typography and fonts, in particular font size and style, layout and balance, with particular reference to designing on-screen, and graphics and logos, focusing on the need for an original angle. Colour considerations, proofing and printing were also covered. Throughout, the course was highly theoretical, with ample exercises and opportunities for hands-on practice. Comprehensive notes were provided for reference and participants were also given a copy of their completed work on disk.

6 What do you think of the style and tone of these paragraphs? How would you change them to make them more suitable for a report?

> The chap who took the course was Will Render from Cambridge, a bit of an expert who teaches regularly at the centre. He obviously knows a thing or two about DTP and he's not a bad teacher either. He was pretty helpful, happy to bend things to suit us all.
>
> All in all the course was great and I can honestly say I learned quite a lot about DTP. It also got my juices going and gave my confidence a bit of a boost, so that was really good. If you use DTP and haven't ever had any design or software training, what's my advice? Get yourself down to The Training Centre and sign up for the course as quick as you can.

7 Combine the corrected paragraphs from exercises 3–6 and add appropriate subheadings to arrive at a complete report.

Answers and recording scripts

Unit 1
Reading

1 c

2 1 G 'Our goal … high-flier.' (lines 49–51)
   2 A an ambitious … his wife. (lines 1–4)
   3 H Higgins … husbands. (lines 62–64)
   4 A she metamorphosed … events. (lines 5–6)
   5 D They meet … nervous? (lines 28–32)
   6 E In company … code names. (lines 38–39)

3 a 'Don't look like a Christmas tree' (lines 16–17)
   b X
   c restraint at the buffet table (lines 33–34)
   d restraint … on the dance floor (lines 33–34)
   e X
   f X
   g avoid conversations about … religion (lines 43–44)
   h do not interrupt if people are talking about business (lines 44–45)
   i never say how wonderful your spouse is in the corporate world (lines 45–46
   j enjoy corporate events (lines 47–48)
   k Know a little bit about the company (line 48)
   l show some interest (lines 48–49)

4 a block (line 3)   f boost (line 42)
   b coaching (line 15)   g high-flier (line 50)
   c modest (line 26)   h asset (line 68)
   d fee (line 27)   i obliging (line 71)
   e high-profile (line 37)

Grammar

5 1 have found   6 was happening / happened
   2 was burning
   3 have been   7 was being done / would be done
   4 have been
   5 was   8 was experiencing

Vocabulary

6 a adapt   h converted
   b altered   i evolved
   c amended/altered   j fluctuate
   d modified   k revise/alter/amend/modify
   e mutated (also developed)
   f transform   l developed/evolved/metamorphosed
   g metamorphosed/developed

7 a tune   e places
   b hands   f clothes
   c ways   g subject
   d mind

The example, c, d, e and g have no corresponding illustration.

8 a made off with
   b get him down
   c coming up against
   d get these exams over (with)
   e came up
   f get the application form in
   g gets around
   h makes up for
   i getting the message across
   j carrying out
   k get the parcel off
   l come off
   m come up

9 a ✓ ✗ ✗   d ✓ ✗ ✗
   b ✗ ✓ ✓   e ✗ ✗ ✓
   c ✓ ✓ ✗   f ✗ ✗ ✓

Unit 2
Listening

1 1 C   2 A   3 D   4 F   5 B

2 a know   f choice   k open
   b moment   g rise   l put
   c hooked   h swim   m lifetime
   d new   i eye-opener
   e second   j soak

3 a put to the test
      rose to the challenge
      no choice but to
   b soak up the atmosphere
      it was a great eye-opener
      well and truly hooked
   c I didn't know what to expect
      sink or swim
      from that moment on

Grammar

4 1 'm not going to be / won't be
 2 leaves
 3 will / 'll be
 4 will /'ll be packing
 5 's/are opening
 6 are/'re on the verge of
 7 shall
 8 will /'ll be visiting
 9 am / will be
 10 will give
 11 am packing
 12 will be developing
 13 will have acquired
 14 will also be considered
 15 will be / are
 16 will also be expected
 17 will be
 18 will
 19 will move
 20 are likely / are expected
 21 may/could/will have
 22 will remain
 23 breaks
 24 is expected / is likely

5 a years'
 b aunt's
 c woman,
 d Washington D.C.,
 e kitchen,
 f , therefore,
 g her,
 h temporarily,

Vocabulary

6 a by no means
 b within reason
 c on its own merits
 d over the top
 e at odds with
 f in all honesty
 g beyond all expectation
 h out of my control

7 a had no doubt
 b had no problem following
 c had no desire
 d had no qualms
 e have no chance of finishing
 f had no option but
 g had no appeal

Use of English

8 1 apprehension
 2 outnumbering
 3 disquiet
 4 understandable
 5 unwieldy
 6 illogical
 7 powerless
 8 expertise

9 1 for
 2 having
 3 To
 4 owing/thanks/due
 5 out
 6 later
 7 which
 8 said

Speaker 1: I'd never travelled at all as a child. I was 18 when I first went abroad. You see, we'd always had family holidays in our own country. I think Dad knew he couldn't cope with the hassle of taking a big family abroad! But when I was 18 he paid for me to fly to Switzerland for a mountain walking holiday with a touring group. In many ways I didn't know what to expect. I guess I thought flying might be quite scary, but in the event I was actually rather disappointed when we had to get off! On the runway I just couldn't believe the views – we were completely surrounded by snow-capped mountains, and from that moment on, I was well and truly hooked on travel.

Speaker 2: Well, travelling abroad was nothing new for me, as my mother's actually Canadian, so most summers we flew over there and stayed with my aunts and uncles. So my first solo trip wasn't the big deal it might've been. Canada's a long way to go alone when you're 20, but it was second nature to me, really. I just had to organise myself, whereas before it had all been done for me. And that's quite a big step, and you have no choice but to rise to the challenge. It's a case of sink or swim, really. Fortunately, I swam.

Speaker 3: Believe it or not, the first time I actually went independently was a business trip to Russia. I'd been overseas dozens of times with family and friends – always *with* somebody. It was a great eye-opener – the whole thing of airports, planes, connections is a whole lot more intense somehow when it's just you. Make a mistake and you're reliant on yourself to sort it out. And I'd say it also intensifies the whole experience of your trip – maybe because you've got a lot more time to think about it and make your own decisions. You soak up the atmosphere ... the experience of being overseas ... that much more.

Speaker 4: My first time overseas was on an English language course in Australia. It was all so new and exciting for me that I'm not sure I really had any expectations. I went into it with an open mind. I suppose one preconception I had, as a city-dweller – of a vast country with loads of countryside to explore – never really got put to the test. I spent all the time in the city of Perth. And well ... city living is city living pretty much anywhere, isn't it? I'd say your first-time abroad alone is the making of you. It makes you much more independent and confident in your life.

Speaker 5: I'd flown before with my family, but when I was 21 I was a really keen runner, and I saw this advert for a big marathon event in Japan. I thought this was a once-in-a-lifetime opportunity, as everything was organised for you, except of course you had to fly by yourself. I knew Japan was supposed to be a really efficient place where everything works well and runs on time. And once I was there the local organisation was first-class, but unfortunately I couldn't say the same about the trip home, as I had numerous problems with delayed flights and such like.

Unit 3
Reading
1 1 C 2 B 3 D 4 A 5 D 6 A 7 C 8 B
   9 A 10 D

Grammar
2 **a** unless you will fail to meet → unless you fail to meet
   Provided you meet our terms and conditions, there should be no problem in arranging that loan for you.

  b would happen → (should) happen
   Should you happen to notice anything strange, kindly make a note of it for me.

  c had → would have
   If jetlag were a figment of the imagination, air travellers would have no problems on arrival at their destination.

  d should cause → can cause
   Given that the sun can cause permanent damage to your eyes, you shouldn't look directly at it.

  e would be heading → will be heading
   If we don't pay more attention to environmental issues, this planet will be heading for destruction.

  f would be able → will be able
   If you stay calm, we will be able to assess the situation quickly.

  g hadn't ever survived → would never have survived
   Without luck on our side, we would never have survived the storm and returned safe and sound.

  h is → will be
   As long as there is a red sky at night, it will be fine the next day.

  i must → will
   Provided you don't spend long periods of time above 5500 metres, you shouldn't/won't experience the ill effects of altitude.

  j didn't persevere → hadn't persevered
   But for your perseverance with your research, / But for the fact that you persevered with your research, you wouldn't have this wonderful evidence to support your theory now.

  k took → take
   As long as you take time to acclimatise when you arrive in a hot country, you won't be asking for trouble.

  l haven't worn → don't wear
   On condition that you don't wear those ridiculous trousers, I'll agree to come to the party.

Vocabulary
3 **a** ways
  b actions
  c conduct
  d bearing
  e reaction
  f demeanour
  g habits

4 **a** affect → effect
  b loose → lose
  c raise → rise
  d practise → practice
  e ansestors → ancestors
  f industrious → industrial
  g alternate → alternative
  h Beside → Besides; experiences → experience

5 **a** sign
  b sight
  c feeling
  d suspicion
  e omen
  f sense
  g intuition

6 **a** guilt
  b tedium
  c rage
  d frustration
  e fears
  f disgust

Use of English
7 1 C 2 B 3 D 4 A 5 D 6 C 7 A 8 B

Unit 4
Listening
1 1 C 2 B 3 A 4 B 5 C 6 C

2 1 d 2 a 3 f 4 e 5 h 6 g 7 c 8 b

3
bland F	moist T	tasteless F
creamy T/F	mushy T	watery T/F
delectable F	overripe T	
fibrous T	palatable F	
grainy T	pulpy T	
insipid F	sharp F	
mild F	stale F/T	

Grammar

4 Where alternative answers are given, the first alternative is the one that is used in the original book.

Be careful not to over-use *used to*, as this may not sound very natural.

1 informed
2 dates/dated back
3 wrote
4 was apparently observed / could apparently be observed
5 just appeared / would just appear / just used to appear
6 would be preceded / was preceded
7 would all be sitting / were all sitting
8 had just caught
9 is
10 (would) suggest
11 is
12 all brought / would all bring / all used to bring
13 used to dangle / would dangle / dangled
14 rode
15 set
16 would assemble / used to assemble
17 was
18 was
19 would begin / used to begin
20 (had) opened up
21 always filled / would always fill / always used to fill
22 could
23 might/would bring OR might/would have brought

Vocabulary

5
a devoured
b chew
c munching
d bolt
e dined
f polished off (*devoured* would also be possible here)

6
a quenching
b watering
c food
d range
e fat
f baked
g fry/fried
h thin
i dried
j centred
k bodied
l grown/made

Use of English

7
1 of
2 another
3 most
4 never/not
5 as
6 mean
7 on
8 so

8
1 are thought to have been introduced
2 put his success down to
3 has the highest consumption of coffee of any / has a higher consumption of coffee than any
4 can/could have failed to notice
5 so/as far as to reveal
6 not have been more

Recording script 03

You will hear three different extracts. For questions 1–6, choose the answer (A, B or C) which fits best according to what you hear. There are two questions for each extract.

Extract One

I spent last year working in Beijing and one of my most memorable days off was a visit to the Daxing Watermelon Festival, which takes place every year in May. Chinese farmers from this district, which lies to the south of the city, come together to celebrate their harvest and compete for the best watermelon prize. The watermelons are judged on a combination of factors. Now, I love watermelons and what counts for me is that the fruit is juicy and relatively free of seeds when I bite into it, but for these growers what matters a lot is how heavy their produce is – and there were some mighty specimens on show. The thickness of the skin and how it looks is also a make-or-break issue for the experts, but that's kind of irrelevant to a consumer like me.

There's far more to this event than winning prizes though. I was particularly struck by the training opportunities on offer to farmers and there're things for tourists to engage with too, as well as souvenirs – and watermelons – to purchase. Quite apart from that, the festival provides a venue for business deals with its trade fair. Everyone should attend this festival at least once in their life!

Extract Two

Interviewer: Sabrina, you've been thumbing through some of the titles in a new series, which showcases the best culinary authors down the centuries. What can you tell us about this series?

Journalist: Well, they're concise and straightforward volumes – the perfect antidote to the typical glossy publishing we've been served up for the last couple of decades – you know, big hardbacks with mouth-watering photography, but which are, at the end of the day, thin on content and can even be a bit disappointing from time to time for the creative cook. By contrast, these books open up new vistas, without any illustrations whatsoever, just very informative and often hilarious text.

Interviewer: Sounds intriguing. Can you give us a concrete example?

Journalist: Yes, indeed, though it's hard to pick out just one from the many gems here. I adored reading the 18th-century writer William Verrall, whose *Recipes from the White Hart Inn* are so evocative of another era in cooking – and hygiene standards. He talks about the challenges of cooking without the best implements, describing a frying pan as being 'as black as my hat', and this is refreshingly different from what we're all used to. A few other writers in the series are just as witty, but none comes up with observations like Verrall's. Some of his recipes are strikingly modern in feel and easy to recreate more than 200 years on, so worth trying if you ...

Extract Three

My husband and I took our son Jack and his girlfriend to a very classy restaurant to celebrate their graduation. We were really looking forward to the experience, as we knew from friends that the menu would be special. And it most certainly was. Jack and his girlfriend aren't meat-eaters so they went for an exquisite-looking medley of grilled aubergines, peppers and goodness knows what else served on a bed of couscous. They found it appetising enough but seemed to hanker after my blackened cod, which I must admit tasted heavenly, even if its appearance was less than perfect! My husband relished his extremely tender and well-seasoned steak, but again, I felt the way it was arranged on the plate lacked originality.

We were seated comfortably at a round oak table in the middle of the room, which was done out in subtle shades of blue and cream, all very tasteful, though the general ambience left something to be desired – with so many waiters dashing about over the wooden floorboards, it was hard to hear ourselves speak at times and the net result was a tiny bit soulless. Still, the food lived up to our expectations and was worth every penny.

Unit 5
Reading

1 1 A 2 D 3 C 4 B 5 C 6 D

Grammar

2

Noun	Countable	Uncountable	Noun	Countable	Uncountable
advice	✗	✓	machinery	✗	✓
appliance	✓	✗	money	✗	✓
business	✓	✓	parking	✗	✓
cash	✗	✓	preference	✓	✓
clothing	✗	✓	produce	✗	✓
competition	✓	✓	product	✓	✗
complaint	✓	✓	promotion	✓	✓
equipment	✗	✓	publicity	✗	✓
experience	✓	✓	right	✓	✓
furniture	✗	✓	shopping	✗	✓
information	✗	✓	success	✓	✓

3 a some/the furniture
   b appliances
   c a complaint / (some) complaints
   d successes
   e a promotion
   f parking
   g a preference / any preference(s)
   h The publicity
   i (any) cash
   j business
   k (Some) Businesses
   l a competition / (some) competitions
   m Competition

4 The following are correct:
   a are   f are   k were
   b are   g is/are   l is/are
   c votes/vote h has/have   m is/are
   d is   i is   n has
   e has/have   j are

Vocabulary

5 1 *complaints:* credit note, defect, faulty goods, legal rights, malpractice, money back, returns
   2 *sales outlets:* department store, Internet, mail order, supermarket, superstore
   3 *aspirations/values:* affluence, image, lifestyle, possessions, status
   4 *people:* consumers, customers, designers, retailers, sales assistants, shopaholics, shoppers

6 a consumer
   b shopping
   c advertising
   d market
   e retail

7 a be in the *right/wrong*
   b be the *right/wrong* way round
   c be within your *rights*
   d catch somebody on the *wrong* foot
   e do the *right/wrong* thing
   f get hold of the *wrong* end of the stick
   g get on the *right/wrong* side of
   h get out of bed on the *wrong* side
   i rub somebody up the *wrong* way
   j strike the *right/wrong* note
   k start off on the *right/wrong* foot
   l the *rights* and *wrongs* of something
   m two *wrongs* don't make a *right*

Use of English

8 1 overtaken
2 homelessness
3 alluring
4 loyalty
5 anxiety
6 unemotional
7 offspring
8 pleasure

Unit 6

Listening

1 1 assessment
2 networking
3 director
4 the Arts Council
5 energy
6 dream
7 rap
8 rowing boat
9 dripping tap

Grammar

2 1 e 2 a 3 d 4 g 5 c 6 h 7 f 8 b

3 a may/might/should score
b might/may seem; can/could/may/might have
c may/might not have given up
d should/could have prepared
e should go / should have gone
f could/can still learn
g shouldn't have said
h must be playing / have played / have been playing
i can't both be learning / learn / have learnt
j could/might have passed
k could/should have let
l can't/couldn't have been cancelled
m can't have practised / have been practising
n must have set
o could/might/may have forgotten
p may/might not have heard

Vocabulary

4 All the words and phrases collocate with *take*.
1 e 2 f 3 c 4 g 5 h 6 a 7 b 8 d

5 a strikingly beautiful
b potentially damaging
c obscenely wealthy
d highly profitable

Use of English

6 1 B 2 B 3 C 4 D 5 A 6 D 7 A 8 C

7 1 nothing   4 in   7 as
2 being   5 as   8 was
3 thing   6 whose

8 1 melancholic   5 automatically
2 fulfil(l)ment   6 unattainable
3 heights   7 longing
4 premature   8 Realistically

Recording script 🔊 04

You will hear a talk by a man called William Bond about his work as a freelance musician. For questions 1–9, complete the sentences with a word or short phrase.
Hello, my name's William Bond, and I'm a freelance musician. I'm going to talk to you about an unusual project I've been involved in, but first a bit of background about myself. Freelance work is obviously really varied. Naturally I've got some private pupils who I give piano or singing lessons to. I also do some work for a local school – I did some consultancy work for them on how to carry out assessment of musical performance, which was very well-paid, and makes up for the times I've been called in at two hours' notice to substitute for a music teacher who's ill! Also, I occasionally give recitals in either piano or organ, but to be honest, unless you're a brilliant professional performer, that kind of work means hundreds of hours' practice and planning for almost no reward, so that side of things you tend to do to make a name for yourself and get contacts in the musical world. You could say it's a form of networking, I suppose, something that all freelance people do in the business world.

Finally, I do a lot of work, more and more in fact, in the world of opera. I get hired by various opera companies as orchestral conductor, or else as the repetiteur – that's the industry name for the person who trains up the singers behind the scenes, erm or even as overall musical director ... in fact that's what I've been doing for the last few weeks. To be honest, these roles can overlap somewhat.

Well, anyway, that brings me nicely to what I was mainly going to talk to you about today, and that's an opera for young homeless people I did last year. What happened was, I heard about a charity organisation which operates a day centre cum night hostel for homeless people in a northern city. I volunteered to do some music therapy workshops – you know, expressing yourself through music. Well, I got talking with the manager of the centre and we came up with an idea – to stage an opera created and performed by the homeless people themselves. She then put this proposal to a body called the Arts Council, and to our surprise, they agreed without hesitation to fund the whole project.

So that's what we did – a local poet called Jennifer Matthews worked with the guys, getting them to come up with ideas for lyrics and storylines and then she went away and turned it all into a script. I did the same with the music – transforming their ideas into something workable which fitted with the lyrics. Often what I'd get from them was, say, a first line of a song which served as a kind of prompt for me to follow or sometimes they might just give me a particular mood that a song should convey, or 'energy' to use their actual term for it. That's the way of working we established, with me agreeing to respect their wishes as far as possible and they in turn leaving me to use my expertise to knock it all into shape.

It was actually one of the most challenging things I've ever done, rather bizarre to be honest, because a lot of the ideas in the storyline were so surreal they sounded like they were something out of a dream and I had somehow to put it all within the framework of music for classical theatre. Also, what they wanted as individuals was of course very subjective and this led to a very eclectic mix, from R and B music to garage music to goodness knows what! If I exposed them to some classical stuff, I in turn learnt a lot about rap – which let's just say I hadn't exactly had occasion to deal with before, but which I rather took to after a while. So quite an eye-opener for me.

Anyway, together Jennifer and I developed the opera partly on thematic lines. For example, we noticed that water happened to feature heavily in the guys' ideas, which were fantastically imaginative! One guy called Dave did a song about someone standing on a beach and watching a pirate ship, and another called Lewis about what it would be like to be in a rowing boat all alone, surrounded by deep blue water. There was a clear connection here. So we backed these two pieces together and accompanied them with a background track that had all kinds of water noises such as a storm at sea and rain on a roof, which I thought was especially effective. It opened with a dripping tap and that went down really well with everyone watching. Clever stuff, eh? Now, moving to the special effects ...

Unit 7
Reading
1 1 F 2 B 3 H 4 A 5 G 6 C 7 E

Grammar
2 1 produced
   2 introduced
   3 considered
   4 offering
   5 Used / Having been used
   6 using
   7 resorting
   8 Having studied
   9 going on
   10 coined
   11 bent
   12 securing

Vocabulary
3 a ✓ ✗ ✓   d ✗ ✓ ✓
   b ✓ ✓ ✗   e ✓ ✓ ✗
   c ✗ ✓ ✓

4 a perceived
   b grasp
   c foresee
   d behold
   e distinguish
   f visualised
   g glimpsed
   h envisage
   i conceive

Use of English
5 1 must be / has to be despatched today without
   2 gone downhill since it changed / since changing
   3 youth, I had no difficulty (in)
   4 longer took any notice of her mother's constant
   5 appalling behaviour, it is doubtful whether/if Geoff will
   6 their play (that) they were bound to win

6 1 A 2 C 3 B 4 A 5 A 6 B 7 B 8 D

Unit 8
Listening
1 1 B 2 A 3 C 4 A 5 B 6 A

Use of English
2 1 opposed   5 any
   2 that   6 made
   3 would   7 of
   4 around/round 8 course

3 1 B 2 B 3 D 4 C 5 D 6 D 7 C 8 A

Grammar
4 a Scarcely had they joined the freeway when/than the traffic ground to a halt.
   b Not until last month did the council start showing interest in the redevelopment scheme.
   c Never before has the city received such imaginative proposals.
   d Seldom is government investment in public transport remotely adequate.
   e Hardly had the new transport network been open when/than a number of similar schemes were announced in cities around the country.
   f Only once have I seen such deprivation and that was in slums that are now demolished.
   g Rarely do/will/can town centre redevelopments achieve a harmonious balance between old and new.
   h Only after the minister (had) finished his tour of inspection did he make his pronouncement.

5 **a** So stressful is city life becoming that more and more people are seeking alternatives.

b Under no circumstances should residents take matters into their own hands.

c Little was the mayor aware that a petition signed by 50,000 people was about to land on his desk.

d On no account should you believe everything property developers will tell you.

e Not only was unemployment already a problem, but further job losses were also on the way.

f In no way did they want to jeopardise the success of the scheme.

g Not one councillor accepted the invitation to observe the development.

h Little did she expect the demolition work to start so quickly, and neither did I.

Vocabulary

6 **a** has no place in
   b a place of my own
   c no place for a
   d a place in history
   e his heart's in the right place
   f go in my place
   g in the first place

7 **a** lose   **d** change   **g** take
   b save   **e** fall
   c take   **f** hold

8 a densely populated area
   a deep-rooted fear
   a world-famous pianist
   a long-winded explanation
   a labour-saving device
   a slow-moving vehicle
   a long-serving member of staff
   a money-making venture

9 1 transport
   2 offers
   3 air
   4 standards
   5 road-users
   6 burden
   7 hour
   8 departure
   9 flow

Recording script 05

You will hear three different extracts. For questions 1–6, choose the answer (A, B or C) which fits best according to what you hear. There are two questions for each extract.

Extract One

Man: Recently I went back to the city where I grew up, and saw the old family home again after 25 years. The great thing about it then was the city was small and we were just a couple of kilometres from the city centre and yet also about the same distance from very pleasant countryside. But now you can see the city's sprawled outwards – there's a motorway and a new suburban development, as others have observed. So now that I have a family of my own, I'm beginning to look quite nostalgically to that era, as I think we had the best of both worlds then in terms of our location.

Woman: I think city life's getting more and more fraught in this country. People are getting sick to the back teeth of all the hassle of urban living – not least the semi-permanent gridlock – and look through rose-tinted spectacles at other less populated parts of the country. Where I live, up in the north, there's tons more space and fantastic air quality, but there's also high unemployment. The money's in the south – that's where all the jobs and development are. It's a situation with no answer really. There's no happy medium.

Extract Two

Man: What do you think about the Regal Hotel? It's certainly a majestic old building.

Woman: It is, and that's the image they try to project, but frankly I think they hide behind that dignified façade and get away with murder … the management there.

Man: Really?

Woman: Yes, there's a stately air about it, but stately easily becomes decrepit. The building's definitely seen better days and you get the feeling they rather paper over the cracks, as it were.

Man: I see. And what about the staff? They're famously well-mannered, I thought.

Woman: To the point of being obsequious. They fawn all over you, which always makes me feel thoroughly uncomfortable in fact, especially at breakfast time. It reminds me of the master and servant thing, whereas I'd much rather just go and help myself to what I want.

Man: A self-service thing, or a buffet … ?

Woman: Yes, then it'd all be much quicker and I wouldn't have to keep on saying 'thank you' umpteen times.

Extract Three

Woman: So do you still run a car now you live in the centre of town?

Man: I do, but to be honest it's a liability. The street's so narrow you can virtually say goodbye to any chance of ever getting out at busy times.

Woman: Have they not heard of a one-way system?

Man: Apparently not. There are cars permanently parked on both sides of the street, so it's a recipe for chaos really.

Woman: So you must be really lucky to have a parking space.

Man: Well, you'd think so, but actually it's often counter-productive to use your car. If I ever move mine, I know there'll be no spaces by the time I get back. It's completely crazy!

Woman: So the irony is, as a car owner you're better off using public transport! But I don't really understand. I mean, do you not have a parking permit?

Man: I do, and permits are only for residents, but the thing is, you're not actually assigned to a particular space, and that's perhaps where the system falls down.

Woman: Oh, I see. So your documentation means you can park anywhere in the street. Yes, that does sound likely to cause problems. And is it also that there are more permits than spaces?

Man: Yes, because some residents are also allowed a visitor's permit – people who are elderly or need help. Not that I begrudge them that – they couldn't manage without it – but it does swell the numbers.

Unit 9
Reading

1 1 C 2 D 3 A 4 B 5 D 6 A 7 C 8 A
   9 D 10 C

Use of English

2 1 objection to me/my taking the afternoon
   2 knowledge (that) there is a ban on smoking / a smoking ban
   3 did he know (that) his wife was about
   4 must have misheard him / what he said
   5 does a contemporary painting receive so
   6 offence at being accused of

Vocabulary

3 *Suggested negative characteristics*
   Horse: ruthless, selfish, unfeeling
   Goat: dissatisfied, insecure, irresponsible, pessimistic, undisciplined, unpunctual

Monkey: long-winded, unfaithful, untruthful, untrustworthy
Rooster: boastful, extravagant, mistrustful, pedantic, pompous, short-sighted
Dog: cynical, introverted, stubborn
Pig: gullible, materialistic, naïve, non-competitive

4 a Dog – noble, courageous, prosperous, devoted, selfless, introverted, stubborn
   b Pig – naïve, gullible, materialistic, scrupulous, sincere, sociable, loyal
   c Monkey – witty, enthusiastic, inventive, untrustworthy, untruthful
   d Goat – sweet-natured, lovable, dissatisfied, insecure, irresponsible, pessimistic

5 a un   c dis   e ig   g in
   b dis   d im   f un   h in

6 a short   c quick/short   e peace
   b hard   d sweet

7 a semi   b pre   c out   d self

What sign are you?
Dragon: 31.1.76–17.2.77   17.2.88–5.2.89
Snake: 18.2.77–6.2.78   6.2.89–26.1.90
Horse: 7.2.78–27.1.79   27.1.90–14.2.91
Goat: 28.1.79–15.2.80   15.2.91–3.2.92
Monkey: 16.2.80–4.2.81   4.2.92–22.1.93
Rooster: 5.2.81–24.1.82   23.1.93–9.2.94
Dog: 25.1.82–12.2.83   10.2.94–30.1.95
Pig: 13.2.83–1.2.84   31.1.95–18.2.96
Rat: 2.2.84–19.2.85   19.2.96–6.2.97
Ox: 20.2.85–8.2.86   7.2.97–27.1.98
Tiger: 9.2.86–28.1.87   28.1.98–15.2.99
Rabbit: 29.1.87–16.2.88   16.2.99–4.2.2000

Grammar

8 1 Furthermore   5 What's more
   2 Consequently   6 on the contrary
   3 Having said that   7 In short
   4 even though   8 Likewise

9 a ironing; putting / to put
   b taking; working
   c to improve
   d being; being / to be
   e to defuse; avoid getting
   f to practise doing; using
   g to embark; to suggest; to see / seeing
   h meeting
   i to stay
   j get; trying to clean; get
   k to buy; to spend
   l lying
   m reading
   n to phone

Unit 10

Listening

1 1 D 2 A 3 D 4 B 5 B

2 project an image · a sense of belonging
update a logo · cultural icons
commercial transaction · political controversy

Use of English

3 1 D 2 C 3 B 4 A 5 B 6 A 7 C 8 D

4 1 tore/ripped
2 then
3 in
4 learnt/learned

5 whose
6 had/produced
7 on
8 although/though/but

5 1 necessarily
2 prosperity
3 unequally
4 underpinned

5 ensure
6 poverty
7 afresh
8 strength

Grammar

6 a spoke / could speak
b to enrol
c would try; would enjoy
d were
e didn't/wouldn't keep
f had had; would have been able
g would have passed; had worked
h was/were
i was/were
j hadn't agreed
k was
l sought
m to start / we (etc.) started
n had been done; had
o asked / had asked
p to have moved / to move; ran

Vocabulary

7 1 emotions
2 development
3 standards
4 inequality

5 forces
6 transport
7 integration
8 good

8 a turnover
b turn-out
c to turn (somebody) away

d to turn in
e downturn
f turn-off

9 a way b events c gave d good e every f twists

Recording script 06

You will hear part of a discussion programme in which a businessman called David and a linguist called Ivana are speaking about the theme of symbols. For questions 1–5, choose the answer (A, B, C or D) which fits best according to what you hear.

David: Well, as you know, Ivana, my line of business is marketing. And there's a lot of symbolism there. Success often comes down to who's projected the most successful image to the public, right? So … companies spend millions on updating their logos to suggest a company with class, … or tradition, … or innovative ideas.

Ivana: So this is really brand symbolism you're talking about.

David: Exactly. Now in my company, we looked into how we could reach out to our customers on an emotional level with something very positive and familiar. And we came up with the idea of incorporating a tick sign into our logo. So in time we hope this symbol will come to represent our brand.

Ivana: Yes, I was reading about this. Apparently, the best brands symbolise something beyond merely a commercial transaction, though – they really connect to an idea that resonates with people, something cultural maybe, so that people really get a sense of belonging.

David: Mm, interesting stuff!

Ivana: And it's also often said that modern life is full of symbols of globalisation – popular cultural icons like Madonna and Coca-Cola. I'd argue that even the Internet itself is a symbol of globalisation, because of the inter-connectedness that it brings to everything in life nowadays.

David: Mm, point taken. On social websites you can interact with the whole world within minutes. In the same breath I'd also mention big global sporting events like The World Cup and the Olympic Games, symbols of sport bringing friendship and happiness between nations.

Ivana: They've also brought their fair share of political controversy, but perhaps that's just me being cynical.

David: No, you're right. There's a long history of various countries using such events for political ends. But I also think people are wise to this, more and more. In any case, these events always seem to turn out very successful, even if you can doubt the intention behind them.

Ivana: But my subject, language, also strikes me as highly symbolic. Because often words have a deeper significance than their purely literal meaning.

David: Right … for example?

Ivana: OK, well, if I say that so and so can run as fast as the wind, I don't really mean that – it's just a way of speaking. So the wind becomes a symbol of the person's speed.

David: Yes ... it's like if you say something like 'a steady stream of people trickled down the hillside'. I think that one's technically a metaphor, isn't it?

Ivana: You're right. And this is a feature of language in general, although the speaker wouldn't think of it as symbolic. But then *writers* do consciously make use of strong personal symbols – the novelist Charles Dickens used the image of fog to symbolise the confusion of the legal profession in London, for example.

David: I see.

Ivana: But there's also a wider point. Language can be a symbol for culture. Obviously people think differently in different cultures and their language reflects their different beliefs. There are words in some languages that don't have an equivalent in other languages.

David: Mm ... anyway, moving the discussion on to other walks of life ... what about sport? I play for a weekend hockey team called Walshingham Wolves, and the wolf appears on our club emblem. It's on the badge on our shirt. You get this with sports teams – they take up the symbol of a dragon or a lion or something and that also becomes the club's nickname ... so we're The Wolves. Our supporters say this symbolises the aggressive style of hockey we play, but that's clearly not the case. Basically the whole wolves thing is just about alliteration – the word sounds good alongside Walshingham! Mind you, I suppose if you have a fierce-sounding name then it helps your team spirit and motivation. I couldn't imagine playing for a team called The Lambs!

Ivana: Absolutely! OK, well another aspect of our theme is colour symbolism. There was a thing on the news recently about how in this country car insurance companies actually charge more for people with red cars because red symbolises anger and aggression, so they think if you choose a red car it must mean you'll take more risks.

David: That does seem completely over the top to me ... my neighbour's labelled more of a risk than me because of the paint on his vehicle! ... Actually, come to think of it, I'm sure I've heard that red cars attract *lower* insurance here because a red car is highly visible in different weather conditions.

Ivana: That just shows how illogical it all is.

David: I suppose the point really is ...

Unit 11
Reading

1 1 C 2 B 3 A 4 C 5 B 6 A

Grammar

2 **a** immensely/deeply
   b deeply/~~absolutely~~; extremely/rather
   c ~~utterly/entirely~~ extremely/fairly/highly/pretty/quite/rather/really/very
   d woefully/~~fairly~~; grossly/~~greatly~~
   e absolutely/~~completely~~; extremely/pretty
   f really/~~eminently~~; pretty/quite; entirely/~~mainly~~
   g rather/utterly; completely/quite
   h ~~highly/woefully~~ extremely/fairly/pretty/quite/rather/really/very; quite/really
   i ~~fairly~~/absolutely; utterly/~~immensely~~

Vocabulary

3 **a** (un)arguable, argumentative
   b awesome, awful
   c (in)defensible, defensive, defenceless
   d fearsome, fearful, fearless
   e (un)forgettable, forgetful
   f (un)imaginable, imaginary, (un)imaginative
   g momentary, momentous
   h restive, restful, restless
   i sensible, (in)sensitive, nonsensical, sensuous, senseless
   j (un)usable, useful, useless

4 **a** awesome
   b indefensible (also insensitive)
   c fearsome
   d forgetful
   e imaginary
   f momentous (also useful)
   g restive
   h nonsensical/senseless
   i useless

5 **a** highly questionable
   b comparatively rare
   c heavily biased
   d deceptively simple
   e blindingly obvious
   f radically reformed
   g ridiculously cheap

6 **a** sacrifice
   b explanation
   c happiness
   d strength
   e fulfilled
   f crucial
   g malnutrition
   h atmosphere
   i professionally
   j separate
   k innocent

Use of English

7 1 is/being   4 far   7 price
   2 whom   5 once 8 end
   3 best   6 my

8 **a** like
   b making; despite; other
   c ahead/forward; sense
   d Had

Unit 12

Listening

1 1 C 2 E 3 H 4 G 5 A 6 H 7 E 8 B
   9 A 10 F

Grammar

2 **a** must be worn
  b must be extinguished
  c must be kept / are to be kept
  d must/should be switched off
  e are permitted
  f is reserved; will be removed

3 *Suggested answers*
  b … conflicting messages are received by the central nervous system …
  c Motion is sensed by the brain …
  d … the input from all three pathways is coordinated by the brain.
  e … there is thought to be …
  f It is hypothesized that …
  g … is ceased/stopped/withdrawn/discontinued etc.
  h The inner sense of balance is reorientated by this visual reaffirmation of motion.
  i … by which means adverse effects of the conflict between vision and balance are reduced.

Vocabulary

4 All 12 verbs mean *cut*.

Across	*Down*
hack	slash
slice	saw
lacerate	slit
excise	dissect
incise	chop
trim	sever

```
A Z S D H A C K
H S L I C E H S
S A I S I C O E
S W T S K U P V
L A C E R A T E
A E X C I S E R
S O H T I P L B
H O I N C I S E
P T R I M W Y S
```

5 **a** hack   **e** slashed   **i** sawing
  b slit   **f** slice   **j** severed
  c trimming   **g** incised   **k** excised
  d dissect   **h** chopped

6 **a** out   **g** off
  b down to   **h** out
  c off   **i** up into
  d across   **j** down
  e back/down on   **k** across/through
  f in   **l** through

7 **a** screw   **d** machine   **g** years
  b edge   **e** fuse
  c wavelength   **f** test

8 **a** firing on all cylinders
  b It's not rocket science
  c put a spanner in the works
  d pushes all the right buttons
  e ran out of steam
  f to hammer the point home

Use of English

9 1 passionately   6 uncompromising
  2 complexity   7 incomprehensibility/ incomprehension
  3 literary
  4 expectations   8 uninitiated
  5 exemplified

10 1 being required to take on / assume too
  2 takes a very brave man / someone (very) brave to do
    OR takes a lot of bravery/courage to do
  3 to be seen to be
  4 to cut down (on) the number/amount

Recording script 🔊 07

You will hear five short extracts in which different people are talking about the Internet.
Look at Task 1. For questions 1–5, choose from the list (A–H) what each speaker's attitude is towards the Internet.
Now look at Task 2. For questions 6–10, choose from the list (A–H) what each speaker currently uses the Internet for most.
While you listen, you must complete both tasks.

Speaker 1: I've always known that the Internet was essential for my work, and I'm on email fairly regularly. I'd say over the past year or two, though, I've become much more open to its many other uses, not least online shopping, which I'm totally addicted to. As I've got a bit more hands-on with the net, the last thing I've moved to is online banking; the fact is, I've always felt that if hackers can get into the top-secret military systems, they're not going to have much problem finding out my bank details. Anyway, I have now signed up on the understanding that the system is foolproof, without being 100% convinced.

Speaker 2: I'm well and truly incapable of seeing any point in constantly networking socially, often with people who you wouldn't give the time of day to if you met them in the street, to give insignificant details about what you've been doing today – as if anyone cares except yourself. However, I will say I have used a friend's page to track down an old friend, so perhaps there's a silver lining in that particular cloud! One thing I do use it regularly for is checking train times – I often have meetings on the other side of the country in connection with work. I can buy my ticket on the train, though.

Speaker 3: Yeah, I use it a lot. I'm forever checking out the last match report for the team I support. I go all over the country to watch them in my spare time. I also surf occasionally for money tips – you know, which shares are doing well. Not that they're always right! You can do all sorts of things on the Internet nowadays. Though whether that's a good thing is another matter. It's completely unregulated, and with that comes undesirable aspects to it … but that's only to be expected, I suppose. On balance I'd say it's probably a force for good. It'll be interesting to see what it looks like ten years from now.

Speaker 4: I think it's astounding the sheer amount of useful information you can now access at the push of a button. It's way beyond my comprehension. I also get completely thrown when technical messages appear on the screen requiring an instant decision – I'm never in a position to make one! Some of it isn't for me – I can't express any enthusiasm for chat rooms, for one thing. But I do often browse the net and only this morning I subscribed to an online cycling magazine. What I find it invaluable for, though, is investigating background issues to do with the companies I devise and run training courses for.

Speaker 5: Well I'm a record producer and I seem to have spent most of my last week online listening to various girls singing. It's all for my old boss in return for something she did for me! I'll be pleased when it's over and done, as I'm not earning a penny from it! One thing that does really annoy me about the Internet is the way it encourages anybody and everybody to make uninformed comments that can be read anywhere in the world. People give their opinions, often in bad English, or else seem to be experts when in fact they've just copied something they've seen on a reputable site. There's no way of stopping this, but technically it's illegal!

c Liz Newman, a mother of three, mused that we live / lived / were living in a world surrounded by concrete and she sometimes wondered what she could do about the environment. She concluded that she could at least sort her trash.

d Recycling specialist David Dougherty questioned why you would cut down a tree to make a newspaper with a lifetime use of just over 20 minutes, then bury it, when you could use it six times over, then burn what's left to create energy. He insisted we had to make recycling a natural part of the economy so that it would become a part of our lifestyle. He reckoned that, of all the environmental concerns that had come up through the years, this was the most personal. In his view, people were uncertain what they could do about saving whales or the rain forest. But they could recycle their waste every day of their lives.

Vocabulary

3 1 e   2 g   3 a   4 j   5 h/c   6 c   7 i   8 b/g
   9 d   10 f

4 a devastation   e precipitation
   b backing   f indigenous
   c chuck   g abundant
   d malnutrition

5 b diversify   h pollute
   c conservation   i activists
   d conservationist   j activate
   e humanity/humankind/ k Consumption
     humans   l consumer
   f humanitarian   m donations
   g pollutant   n donor

Use of English

6 1 other   5 some
   2 that   6 often/frequently
   3 without   7 over
   4 every/all/any   8 until

Unit 13
Reading
1 1 C 2 E 3 H 4 F 5 A 6 D 7 G

Grammar
2 a Industry consultant William Moore acknowledged that recycling paper would never completely eliminate cutting down trees, but said it could mean cutting fewer trees.

   b Harold Barrington, a recycling enthusiast from Oklahoma, said that he had built a machine that made/makes petroleum out of old tyres. He claimed he had produced / to have produced as much as 8,000 litres of crude oil in five hours. Apparently, he had distilled some into gasoline to run his machines and (had) sold the rest to a refinery.

Unit 14
Listening
1 1 B 2 D 3 C 4 A 5 B

2 a animal   d muscle   g exerting
   b point   e ceases   h swings
   c take   f repetitive

Grammar
3 a – Research carried out by **the** Institute of – Respiratory Medicine ***at*** **the** Royal Prince Alfred Hospital in Sydney, Australia, suggests that there is **a** correlation ***between*** the consumption of oily fish and **a/the** reduction ***in/of*** children's risk **of** developing – asthma. New studies are also beginning to make **a** connection ***between*** a deficiency in – omega 3 fatty acids and – depression and – mental illness.

b Jane Clark is **a** state-registered dietician and **the/–** author **of** the *Bodyfoods* series of – books. As **a** teenager she was interested in medicine but wanted to work **with** food instead of – drugs, so she did **a** degree **in** dietetics **at** Leeds University.

c Everyone responds differently **to** food in the morning: some people feel sleepy and unable to function after eating **a** large breakfast, whereas others need **a** hearty breakfast before they embark on **the** day's activities.

d – Chocolate causes your blood-sugar level to rise quickly, which stimulates **the** pancreas to produce – insulin, **a/the** hormone that rapidly brings it **down**. – Fresh fruits give **the** best slow-release energy boost, so increase your fruit intake.

e – Strenuous exercise results **in the** release **of** – endorphines in **the** brain, giving athletes **a** natural 'high'. Some athletes become dependent **on the** effect, but it does not harm them **in** any way.

f Make sure that you drink plenty of – water throughout **the** day to enable all **the** energising vitamins, minerals and slow-release sugars in the food that you eat to be absorbed **by** your body. – Adults should aim to drink two to three litres of – water **a** day.

g It is best to exercise every day. Three days **a** week is **the** absolute minimum. Work out **the** best time of – / **the** day to fit in **an** exercise programme. It is unwise to exercise if you are injured or if you have any form of – fever or **a/–** viral infection such as **a** cold or **the/–** flu.

Vocabulary

4
a avoiding
b trying
c asked
d ignored/avoided; left
e decided; ask
f holding
g looked/searched/read
h enjoy
i beat
j try/attempt
k promised
l spoke to
m get rid of / cut / remove
n affect
o believes in / supports / advises
p claimed/said
q reveal/say
r has
s fight
t imagine

5
a get it off her chest
b up to my ears
c makes my hair stand on end
d head and shoulders above
e all fingers and thumbs
f pulling my leg
g keep me on my toes
h get my head round
i lift a finger

Use of English

6
1 by (only/just) a handful of competitors/runners in its
2 has the makings of
3 paid to my hopes of / any hopes I had of getting/ having
4 dislike to sport on account of being
5 on the understanding (that) it would
6 another word/thing to him it serves

7
1 humiliation
2 endless
3 unwanted
4 unbelievable
5 statements
6 validate
7 disorientation
8 tiredness

Recording script 🔊 **08**

You will hear part of a programme in which a coach called Rob Johnson and a physiotherapist called Donna Davies are discussing health and fitness. For questions 1–5, choose the answer (A, B, C or D) which fits best according to what you hear.

Rob: Nice one Donna! Very amusing!

Donna: Thanks, Rob. Now something I wanted to ask you was … you're a swimming coach. Do you actually think there is a best sport for fitness?

Rob: Are my guys any fitter than boxers or sprinters? Mm. The question's only relevant if you're a member of the public looking to get fit from a starting point of not already being fit. Then, yes, you should look at tapping into some swimming, some running, some gym work – because you'll benefit from all of them. But fitness at a higher level is sports specific. A true swimmer can't train like a boxer and a boxer can't train like a gymnast. And within that, a sprint swimmer is an entirely different animal from a distance swimmer, so who's to say which of them is fitter? Neither can do what the other can, so really at that level it's a complete non-question.

Donna: Yes, that's interesting, and I think you make an important point about what fitness is and what it means. I would add that in the general fitness mass market, what we can see is that there's always been a tendency to equate fitness with how far you can go.

Rob: Yes, an 80-kilometre bike ride is seen as a measure of fitness.

Donna: But without wanting to sound aloof and snooty, it might've taken a whole day's riding on a tip-top racing-style bike, in which case it means almost nothing in terms of fitness. Generally, faster and shorter can be equated with fitter, and casual trainers would probably benefit more from, say, the greater muscle tone that that would bring. Endurance is just one aspect of a much wider picture, but it's the thing that people grab on to.

Rob: Mm. Let me move things on to another aspect of fitness, and that's cross training. That's one of the buzzwords of the moment, and cyclists are off running, and runners are out swimming, and all in the belief it'll help them improve in their own sport. Now if you're just in the general fitness market, and you're not seriously competing in one sport, I'm all for doing it eclectically like that, but if you're a serious cyclist then it's a moot point whether you'll benefit from going off and doing some rowing. Well, you get stronger all round, that's true, but once you get back on your bike, it's back to your leg muscles; and having stronger arms, if it comes with added bulk, is actually going to be a hindrance.

Donna: I agree. For serious sportspeople I think it has potential value in terms of injury prevention, but think of a sprint runner. Now obviously too much sprinting puts a real strain on the body, not least because you're up on your toes all the time, so your feet and legs really take a battering. So understandably some coaches look to incorporate swimming into the training programme. But swim too much and the sprinter will lose some muscle bulk and they'll then have less power to bring to bear on their running. So cross training ceases to be effective if it becomes anything other than something supplementary to your regular training.

Rob: So Donna, as a sports physiotherapist, would you advise people wanting to get fit to head for the gym?

Donna: Each to his own, really. The key thing is what you enjoy and what's going to continue to get you going. I must admit if you're pushing me for a personal view I do baulk a bit at seeing people walking on treadmills in gyms, especially when they can see the hills behind the town from the gym I use. But anyway, the gym is always going to be useful to different people in different ways.

Rob: Yes, clearly.

Donna: I'm actually using the gym to treat a long-distance skier at the moment – not the downhill type, the cross-country variety on the flat. In my view this sport is wonderful for your heart and lungs, but in fact uses a highly repetitive motion that isn't actually natural at all. So there's another issue, predictability. Sports like this are at the top end of predictability in that the muscles do the same relatively confined action again and again. My patient's got a serious over-use injury and we're doing a whole body rehabilitation to strengthen bones and joints. So I'm making him do completely unpredictable muscle movements – things that the likes of gymnasts and wrestlers do.

Rob: Mm. Very interesting!

Donna: So, Rob, you're one of the healthiest individuals I've seen! Do you equate fitness with health?

Rob: That's a hard one.

Donna: I mean, we all know someone to whom sport is complete anathema but who's the very picture of health.

Rob: Mm, we do, but I wonder how old that someone is. I bet you they don't go on being paragons of health well into middle age.

Donna: Maybe, and I suppose those who've taken care of themselves earlier in life do get less problems later on.

Rob: Mm. Then again, over-exerting yourself can no doubt lead to lowered resistance to infection.

Donna: You're not wrong there. So it's swings and roundabouts really.

Rob: I guess so.

Unit 15
Reading
1   1 G   2 C   3 B   4 E   5 H   6 A   7 F

Vocabulary
2   a whereas
    b Indeed
    c On the other hand
    d conversely
    e Likewise
    f by the same token
    g Despite

3   a a ballpark figure
    b working my fingers to the bone
    c it's all doom and gloom
    d my hands are tied
    e keep our heads above water
    f thinking outside the box
    g it's time for a reality check
    h put his money where his mouth is

Grammar
4   1 c   2 e   3 a   4 d   5 b

5   a in order to / so as to
    b for fear that
    c in order not to / so as not to
    d in case / lest
    e so that

6 *There are many possible correct answers here, including these suggestions*

in order to impress his boss.

in case the boss wasn't impressed by his work. / in case the boss thought he was lazy. / in case the boss had noticed he was late that morning.

for fear that the boss wasn't impressed by his work. / for fear that his boss would think he was lazy.

so as not to lose time on his important project. / so as not to give the impression that he was lazy.

Use of English

7 1 D 2 A 3 B 4 C 5 A 6 D 7 A 8 B

Unit 16
Listening
1 1 F 2 C 3 H 4 B 5 E 6 D 7 H 8 A
   9 F 10 E

2 a literary   h publication
   b figurative   i descriptive
   c contradictory   j tendency
   d inconsistencies   k curiosity
   e personalise   l characterisation
   f seamlessly   m strengths; portraying
   g creativity   n atmospheric

Grammar

3 a Even though   i Whereas
   b However   j In spite of
   c Although   k Despite / In spite of
   d Much as   l As a result of
   e as/though   m As
   f As well as   n Although
   g However   o Much as
   h As; as (OR: Dramatic p As
     though her plots are …)

Vocabulary

4 a invisible   e lurking   i camouflaged
   b concealed   f masked   j veiled
   c encoded   g shrouded   k secret
   d obscured   h covert   l disguised

5 answer   country   indict   receipt
   business   debt   island   rhyme
   circuit   gnome   listen   salmon
   column   handkerchief marriage   yeoman

6 1 dough   9 mother   17 work
   2 through   10 both   18 ward
   3 heard   11 broth   19 font
   4 bird   12 there   20 word
   5 dead   13 dear   21 go
   6 bead   14 bear   22 cart
   7 meat   15 rose
   8 debt   16 choose

Use of English

7 1 was disappointed, Karen bore him no ill
   2 long I read (for), I always end up
   3 made/became friends with Colin, his behaviour has taken
   4 never fail to bring
   5 to be allowed out in case it got/was
   6 down/out by / because of the daily grind of

Recording script 🔊 09

You will hear five short extracts in which different people are talking about trying to write their first novel.
Look at Task 1. For questions 1–5, choose from the list (A–H) how each person felt during the experience.
Now look at Task 2. For questions 6–10, choose from the list (A–H) what each person learnt.
While you listen you must complete both tasks.

Speaker 1: I tried to do a novel to a carefully thought-out formula. I figured that increasingly people want a lighter read these days, as they don't have time to read enormously long books. So, I kept it light and easy with self-contained chapters. The publisher I sent it to applauded my well-reasoned attempt to do something different, but said that it didn't cut much ice. That was a valuable lesson for me. It wasn't that hard to write, and I seemed to rattle on at a fair old pace, but one thing that did trouble me was writing descriptive passages. That's always been one of my failings, to be honest, and I could sense it myself when I re-read it.

Speaker 2: From the outset I decided to employ a friend who would comment on the material. What she picked up was that I was falling into the trap of 'telling' things too clearly and directly, doing all the work for the reader. That had never occurred to me. Overall I have no regrets about doing the novel, even if it was simply a labour of love. But I would say at times I felt it was an isolating experience, when I'd go whole days without feeling part of the world at large. At times I was tempted to put in something that would shock the reader, but in the end I'm glad I didn't resort to this.

Speaker 3: I knew more or less what kind of novel I wanted to write, and I spent six months reading up on published novels on similar themes. See, I had it all ruthlessly planned! But that approach had its drawbacks – at times I was probably too influenced by them, to be honest. I don't think I ever suffered from 'writers' block' as it's called. If anything, it was the opposite for me: I noticed early on that I had a tendency to ramble and get a bit long-winded. This is something I taught myself to avoid so it never got to be a problem. My instinct was that I should keep everything true to the real world, and I think this shines through.

Speaker 4: I knew I had very little chance of getting accepted by a publisher if I sent my work in unsolicited, so I got a literary agent interested by sending him a couple of chapters. He agreed to comment on what I'd done so far, and his point was that there seemed to be some very bland parts where I was just going through the motions. I put this down to a daily nine-to-five working schedule I'd imposed on the task, and agreed to free this up. Later on, I got to one bit which, although I was very pleased with it, was rather contentious. And I must admit it did leave me wondering how it would be received by readers.

Speaker 5: I made a conscious effort to write from the heart and put my own experiences into the work ... within a pre-ordained framework I'd worked out. Even so, at times the manuscript seemed to develop a mind of its own and go off in a direction I hadn't envisaged. It was exciting to get swept along, but in a way I didn't really want it to happen. It was my first attempt at a novel, and it became clear to me that you need a kind of hook to draw the reader in, and you need to keep on repeating this trick to make sure you've got the reader's attention.

Unit 17
Reading
1 1 D 2 C 3 D 4 B 5 D 6 A 7 C 8 A
   9 C 10 D

Grammar
2 a He could not have been more thrilled with your gift.
   b Life in retirement is a good deal easier than going to work every day.
   c There's not as much glamour in the film business as people like to make out.
   d Country life is nowhere near as stimulating as city life.
   e I would sooner not go out on the lake – I am nothing like as good a swimmer as you are.
   f We honestly feel more fulfilled now than ever before.
   g By far the best thing we ever did was (to) move to the country.
   h She looks as young now as she did 10 years ago.
   i Performing on stage was nothing like as scary as I thought it was going to be.
   j They would much sooner walk than go by car.
   k Looking after a small house is not as much work as looking after a large one.
   l Everyone always thinks they would be happier if they had (more) money.
   m All that good living is making them fatter than ever!

3 *Suggested answers*
   a The bigger the boxer, the more powerful his/her/the punches are.
   b The heavier the object, the faster it falls.
   c The warmer the weather, the more lethargic I become.
   d The cleaner the river, the more fish you find (in it).
   e The longer it ferments, the better it tastes.
   f The longer I read, the more my eyes hurt.

Vocabulary
4 a whale (happy)   g tears (unhappy)
   b spring (happy)   h weight (unhappy)
   c blues (unhappy)   i boots (unhappy)
   d world (happy)   j bump (unhappy)
   e moon (happy)   k crest (happy)
   f dumps (unhappy)   l heart (happy)

5 a downcast   f forlorn
   b disheartened   g depressed
   c troubled   h inconsolable
   d mournful   i hurt
   e miserable   j miserable

6 a long and hard   f correct
   b aches and pains   g far and wide
   c read and write   h nearest and dearest
   d correct   i supply and demand
   e each and every   j correct

Use of English
7 1 C 2 D 3 A 4 B 5 D 6 A 7 B 8 C

Unit 18
Listening
1 1 B 2 A 3 A 4 C 5 C 6 A

Vocabulary
2 The word is *free*.
   a free hand   e scot-free   i free spirit
   b walk free   f free-range   j free-
   c set free   g interest-free   standing
   d free time   h free fall

3 autocrat, despot, dictator, tyrant
   elude, escape, evade, flee
   free, liberate, release, reprieve
   captive, convict, jailbird, prisoner
   custodian, guard, keeper, warder
   confinement, detention, imprisonment, incarceration
   a prisoner
   b evade (*escape* would also be correct but stylistically less appropriate)
   c reprieve (also *free, release*)
   d custodian (also *keeper*)
   e correct (also *imprisonment, incarceration, confinement*)
   f correct, though *autocrat* is not disapproving; *despot, tyrant* are

4 **a** in; in　　**e** on　　**i** on
　　b to; in　　**f** behind　　**j** in
　　c on　　　**g** under　　**k** of
　　d at　　　**h** through

Grammar

5 **a** can/may be borrowed
　　b would have phoned; could / had been able to
　　c could/might/would have been injured
　　d ought to have / should have reviewed
　　e might have / could have won
　　f should have been / ought to have been
　　g needn't have stayed / didn't have to stay
　　h ought not to have agreed / shouldn't have agreed; would/might/could be
　　i could not have started
　　j can't/couldn't have left
　　k must have told

Use of English

6 1 A 2 C 3 C 4 D 5 B 6 D 7 D 8 B

7 1 no　　　　4 it/things　　7 as
　　2 myself　　5 most　　　8 too
　　3 by　　　　6 and

8 1 ecstatic　　　　5 graceful
　　2 instinctive　　　6 (re)assurance
　　3 spontaneous　　7 anxieties/anxiety
　　4 assortment　　　8 improvisation

Recording script 🔟

You will hear three different extracts. For questions 1–6, choose the answer (A, B or C) which fits best according to what you hear. There are two questions for each extract.

Extract One

Man: I think you and I, relatively speaking, have got it very easy – cushy jobs, easy lifestyle. A bit of stress, OK. But we've never properly experienced true freedom, because we've never had anything big to struggle against.

Woman: I know what you're saying, but you can still taste freedom in a diluted form. I had an operation in hospital recently and after it I felt a great sense of freedom, release, relief … call it what you will. Just this wonderful feeling that from now on things could only get better.

Man: I guess you're right. I had quite a dilemma a few years ago, when I was in this high-pressure job with a boss I didn't care for. Out of the blue one day my old boss from my previous job rang to ask if I could come back in a more senior role. It meant a considerable pay cut, and a feeling of going back down in the world. The easy thing to do would've been to stay put and avoid any hassle, but in the end I did it. And, as you say, I felt, for want of a better word, a sense of freedom.

Extract Two

It's well documented that I quit my course at the Royal Institute of Music. So I was classically trained, but I broke off with it because my gut instinct was that it wasn't for me. It was all too controlled and mainstream, and I guess I was too much of a rebel. I wanted to take liberties with the rhythm, run with an idea and see where it took me. But you see, I now acknowledge that I couldn't possibly have done this, couldn't have achieved everything I subsequently did in my career, without the background I had. It gave me a launching pad from which to branch off on a different angle. Am I returning to my classical roots? No, it's not a case of me changing because I'm getting older. But perhaps what's changed in me is a willingness to acknowledge my debt a little bit. With today's younger pop stars and composers, what they're schooled in is the idea that it's all about just go out and create, but you see, you can't create in a vacuum. You need a starting point. And for me, that was rejection of the norms, and celebrating the freedom that gave me.

Extract Three

Man: With me is journalist Lucy Waters. Lucy, what are your feelings on the state of press freedom?

Woman: First and foremost, as a journalist, I believe that being free to express yourself is a universal human right. Politicians shouldn't be able to curb it in any way. After all, in a democratic society, there needs to be an open society so that the people can make informed judgements, and they do that with the help of the press. I know journalists have come in for quite a bit of stick recently, as a result of a number of scandals and I can't condone that, but the majority of us do abide by the rules.

Man: What do you think about the rules that are in place at present?

Woman: We're lucky not to face too much censorship. But it's not all plain sailing. In Britain there are libel laws, the Official Secrets Act, not to mention a host of other laws. But at least the police need a court order before they can force us to reveal our sources. There has always been, though, a culture of official secrecy in this country and it took until 2000, with the Freedom of Information Act, for people to legally find out certain information. Amazing, when you think about it.

Unit 19

Reading

1 **1** C **2** C **3** D **4** A **5** D **6** D

Vocabulary

2 **a** chattering   **f** clapped   **k** crunching
   b hummed   **g** plopped   **l** giggling
   c fluttering   **h** hiccupped   **m** slurp
   d beeps   **i** mumbling   **n** rustling
   e thudding   **j** bubbling

3 **a** apparition   **g** instinctive
   b destructive   **h** coincidental
   c illogical   **i** scientific
   d hypnotic   **j** explanation
   e unbelievably   **k** incomprehensible
   f uneasily

Grammar

4 *Suggested answers*

   a He sits alone in his room all day long / He sits all day long alone in his room, painstakingly writing up his findings by hand, mostly on scrap paper and usually in unfathomably long and complex sentences.

   b To my astonishment the fortune-teller's predictions turned out to be uncannily accurate.

   c Strangely enough, although it was practically dark, I was actually feeling quite relaxed as I waited patiently for a glimpse of the apparition, but naturally that changed dramatically when the room went cold all of a sudden / when all of a sudden the room went cold.

   d I've never seen anything look quite so eerie or move so strangely – I was terrified out of my wits!

   e Curiously there hadn't been any further sightings of the ghost in the castle since the previous owner left last summer.

   f He was made up very realistically for the carnival the other day – he looked just like the ghost of an old woman.

   g He always speaks intelligently on the subject of the paranormal, but the talk he was giving later was generally expected to be even better than usual.

   h For some reason the computer in the back office started behaving rather oddly, inexplicably flashing up strangely disturbing messages onto the screen.

Use of English

5 **1** were no limits to the magician's
   2 an open mind when it
   3 went on in that room really gave me
   4 much doubt that/if/whether there's such a / any such
   5 (who is) representing the socialist party is running
   6 glimmer of hope of finalising the deal in

Unit 20

Listening

1 **1** skyline   **6** blowtorches
   2 (college) dance   **7** tour guides
   3 a plank   **8** robotics
   4 (some) careless drivers   **9** distress
   5 balloon

Grammar

2 **a** got; set up
   b having/getting; cleaned
   c had/got; stolen
   d have; deliver (also *get; to deliver*)
   e had; happen
   f got/had; kitted out
   g have; enjoying
   h having/getting; analysed
   i Have; wait (also *Get; to wait*)
   j had/got; laughing
   k have; throwing
   l have; turned into
   m get; to come (also *have; come*)
   n had; fill out (also *got; to fill out*)
   o have; arrested
   p get; to meet
   q got; caught
   r got; finished
   s get; telling
   t got / had got; working / to work (also *had; working*)

Vocabulary

3 **a** droll, facetious, humorous, hysterical, jocular
   b beam, grin, smirk
   c cackle, chuckle, giggle, roar, snigger, snort, titter
   d beam, cackle, chuckle, giggle, grin, roar, smirk, snigger, snort, titter
   e droll, facetious, humorous, hysterical, jocular
   f cackle, chuckle, giggle, roar, snigger, snort, titter
   g cackle (unpleasant to listen to), facetious (inappropriate), smirk (self-satisfied, disapproving), snigger (unkind), snort (can imply derision), titter (when something isn't intended to be funny)

4 **a** a go of   **f** go up   **l** a go at
   b go by   **g** stop at   **m** go off
   c to a stop   **h** stopped up   **n** gone over
   d stop off   **i** gone down   **o** stopping
   e go into (also   **j** going in for   over (also
      over)   **k** a stop to   *off*)

5 agree (*has* doesn't agree with *verbs*)
   a end (*with* is a preposition)
   b start (*And* is a conjunction)
   c split (*to ever split* is a split infinitive)
   d clichés (*like the plague* is a cliché)
   e always (*always* is alliterative here)

f specific (*more or less* is not specific)

g unnecessary (this sentence includes two sets of parenthetical remarks)

h fragments (this is a sentence fragment)

i Contractions (this sentence includes two contractions)

j generalise (this is a generalisation)

k double (*don't use no* is a double negative)

l Avoid (the sentence contains both an ampersand and an abbreviation)

m commas (there are two unnecessary commas in this sentence)

n diminutive (*diminutive* is a big word)

o exclamation (the sentence ends with three exclamation marks)

p correctly (*irregardless* is incorrect)

q apostrophe (the first *it's* does not need an apostrophe, the second *its* does)

r Puns (*groan* is a pun on *grown*)

s Proofread (the word *left* has been omitted between *you* and *any*)

6 a differently from/to
b on the bright side
c taking into account
d with reference to
e at my own risk
f by nature
g point of view on things
h for no reason
i in high demand

Use of English

7 1 as she was, revenge was the last thing
2 daughter's wedding was concerned, nothing was too
3 you (can) turn a blind eye to
4 been on the go since she arrived
5 stopped short of telling her my (true/real)
6 had her car broken into

Recording script 🔊 11

You are going to hear a talk from a woman called Emma Coleman about university student pranks, or practical jokes. For questions 1–9, complete the sentences with a word or short phrase.

Over the years British and American university students in particular have become famous for pranks. These practical jokes can be quite ambitious and high profile, but they're all in good humour and nobody ever gets hurt. Arguably the most ingenious student prank of all time was carried out in June 1958, when the people of Cambridge woke to an unusual sight – a car was perched on a university rooftop, looking for all the world as if it were driving across the skyline. It made the headlines all around the world, leaving police, firefighters and civil defence units battling to work out a way of getting it back down.

Only in the last few years have we learnt the identity of the mastermind behind the stunt: one Peter Davey, an engineering student at Gonville and Caius College, who hatched the plan while looking out of his college bedroom window over to the Senate House roof. Now the Senate House building is used mainly for degree ceremonies, so it's very much in the public eye, and it's situated between Kings College and Gonville and Caius. Peter recruited eleven other students to help realise his plan.

After finding a clapped-out car, an Austin Seven, the group had to tow it through Cambridge to a parking space near the Senate House. They hit on the idea of sticking signs on it advertising a college dance to explain its presence. A ground party manoeuvred the car into position while a lifting party on the Senate House roof hoisted it up using an A-shaped crane constructed from scaffolding poles and steel rope. A third group, the bridge party, passed a plank across the notorious Senate House Leap – a three-metre gap between the roof and a turret window at Gonville and Caius – and helped the lifters ferry across lifting gear comprising three types of rope, hooks and pulleys.

Policemen who heard a commotion as the equipment passed above them questioned some of the ground party but their attention was taken up with some careless drivers nearby and so they left the students alone. The mechanics of the prank baffled onlookers. Three rowers, returning to college after a night on the town, spotted the car swinging about 12 metres up. Goodness knows what it must've looked like in the dark – a tent flapping in the wind, maybe? They were fobbed off with the explanation that it was a tethered balloon. The stunt almost went awry when the team tried to swing the car through the apex of the A-frame, over the Senate House balustrade and it fell on to the roof.

The next day the bizarre sight enthralled crowds of onlookers, and attempts by the authorities to construct a crane to hoist it back down failed. They eventually gave up on that plan and took it to pieces with blowtorches. The Dean of the college had an inkling who was responsible and sent them a congratulatory case of champagne, while maintaining in public he knew nothing of the culprits.

In fact, the shadowy group of engineering students who executed the stunt were until recently never identified and the mystery of how they did it baffled generations of undergraduates. It also provided interesting material for tour guides. Such people must have been rather put out when, 50 years after the great event, in 2008, the group reunited at an anniversary dinner to disclose their identities and reveal how they did it.

It won't surprise you to know, having heard this inventive tale, that many of the group went on to enjoy illustrious careers. Peter Davey was awarded an honorary doctorate after setting up robotics companies, while another, Cyril Pritchett, was a lieutenant colonel in the army. Gonville and Caius officials said the 'renegades' had turned into generous benefactors of the college. Apparently, the reunited group said their only regret was that the car was not left in place for ever!

Well, the story of the Cambridge prank has captured my imagination and I'm in the process of writing a book on the best student pranks ever seen. The only two golden rules of the student prank are that they should cause no lasting damage to any property or any distress to any individual, and that they should surprise and preferably delight those who encounter them. If you have heard of a prank that deserves a wider audience – I'd love to hear from you.

Writing workout 1 Letter

1 1 e 2 i 3 a 4 k 5 g 6 h 7 b 8 f 9 j
    10 c 11 d

3 The order is b, a, d, c, e.

Optional writing task

If possible, show your letter to your teacher. Otherwise, once you have worked through exercises 4–7, compare it with the version in the Key for exercise 7.

4 spontaneous, stereotypical, pleasurable, individual's, relationships

5 1 As
    2 not only
    3 but also
    4 Furthermore
    5 while
    6 as
    7 In my view
    8 namely

6 [1]Recent research [2]suggests that play may be as important for us and other [3]animals as sleeping and dreaming. And no-one would [4]dispute that play is an important part of a [5]healthy, happy childhood. But if play is necessary for the [6]physical and [7]social development of young animals, [8]including humans, what [9]happens if young creatures are [10]prevented from playing or [11]maltreated with the result that their play is [12]abnormal? Their [13]development may also be abnormal. [14]Certainly the [15]behaviour of 'problem dogs' [16]invariably develops through [17]improper games or lack of games when they were young.

7 4 a 5 d 6 c

Dear Sir

Your delightful article on play behaviour among animals is a poignant reminder of just how fascinating wildlife can be. However, it also raises some far-reaching questions on the purpose of play, which the writer failed to discuss. Do mammals and birds gain anything from it, or do they do it just because it feels good?

I tend to think of play as spontaneous behaviour that has no clear-cut goal and does not conform to a stereotypical pattern and your article would seem to encourage this view. To me the purpose of play is simply play itself; it appears to be pleasurable. But play also has benefits: it is key to an individual's development, social relationships and status.

As a dog-owner, I know play is vital for proper development in dogs: games of keep away, chase and tug-of-war not only develop physical abilities but also help the animals attain social status by establishing superior mental and physical skills. Furthermore, play, while it often mimics aggression, as in the article, is one form of defence used to defuse potential confrontations. In my view, ritualised play in humans, namely sports, serves an identical purpose.

Recent research suggests that play may be as important for us and other animals as sleeping and dreaming. And no-one would dispute that play is an important part of a healthy, happy childhood. But if play is necessary for the physical and social development of young animals, including humans, what happens if young creatures are prevented from playing or maltreated with the result that their play is abnormal? Their development may also be abnormal. Certainly the behaviour of 'problem dogs' invariably develops through improper games or lack of games when they were young.

Today millions of children spend endless hours watching television and playing computer games instead of playing with one another. Maybe they should take a lead from the animals.

Yours faithfully

(316 words)

Writing workout 2 Review

1 a, c, d, e, f, g, h, i. A review should only include a brief summary of what is being reviewed, not full details (b), and personal anecdotes and hearsay (j) are also inappropriate.

2 Neither text is a complete review, but Text B is compiled from authentic review material. This is clear from its reference to a specific playwright/play/production, the brief descriptive synopsis and the evaluative comments / expressed opinions. Text A is from a biographical entry on Pinter in *The Oxford Companion to English Literature*.

Optional writing task

If possible, show your review to your teacher. Otherwise, once you have worked through exercises 3–7, compare it with the version in the Key for 7.

3 1 allusions
2 dense
3 like chasing a drop of water through a fountain
4 Directed
5 playwright
6 packed

4 1 seeming   5 shabby/seedy
2 hidden   6 inner
3 imposing   7 sharp
4 seedy/shabby

5 *Suggested answer*
The two central characters are seeming opposites, bound together by a hidden affinity. Hirst is a successful literary man living in a really imposing house in Hampstead. He invites Spooner, a seedy pub worker from Chalk Farm, to his house. Hirst's life represents everything that Spooner has dreamed of. For Hirst, Spooner stands for what he might have become. Not that it's just about success and failure. Hirst's success has turned to ashes. He is a heavy drinker, living in a state of moral paralysis. But it is only outwardly that Spooner embodies what he has escaped from. The shabby guest is also an emanation of the well-dressed host's inner emptiness. There is a sense of tragic waste in the play, of things left undone. At the same time there is some sharp and perceptive comedy. This new production does equal justice to both aspects.

6 1 terrific   5 frosty
2 superlative   6 uninspiring
3 harmless   7 ingratiating
4 cunning

7 *Suggested answer*

On the page, Harold Pinter's *No Man's Land* is enough to give the reader a panic attack. The literary allusions are so dense, the dislocation of character so mysterious that pinning down what's going on is like chasing a drop of water through a fountain. But it's striking how little this matters in performance. Directed by the playwright, at London's Lyttleton Theatre, this most metaphysical of Pinter's plays is immediate, fully fleshed and packed with social detail.

The two central characters are seeming opposites, bound together by a hidden affinity. Hirst is a successful literary man living in a really imposing house in Hampstead. He invites Spooner, a seedy pub worker from Chalk Farm, to his house. Hirst's life represents everything that Spooner has dreamed of. For Hirst, Spooner stands for what he might have become.

Not that it's not just about success and failure. Hirst's success has turned to ashes. He is a heavy drinker, living in a state of moral paralysis. But it is only outwardly that Spooner embodies what he has escaped from. The shabby guest is also an emanation of the well-dressed host's inner emptiness. There is a sense of tragic waste in the play, of things left undone. At the same time there is some sharp and perceptive comedy. This new production does equal justice to both aspects.

The leads are terrific. Corin Redgrave as Hirst and John Wood as Spooner both give superlative performances. Wood, on the surface all genial and harmless, also comes over as disturbingly cunning and manipulative while Redgrave's frosty arrogance is brilliantly done. Though Danny Dyer is uninspiring as one manservant, Andy de la Tour has the ingratiating manner of the other servant down to perfection.

I must confess I found the temperature of the play dropped somewhat in the second half, but overall it was a powerful and satisfying evening.

(311 words)

Writing workout 3 Essay

1 1 b 2 a 3 b 4 a 5 b

2 *Possible ideas*
For
• It is human nature to want to explore and discover new things.
• It is exciting and inspiring to learn more about the universe and our place in it, and possibly to understand more about the origins of life.
• Technological developments that are the result of the space programme may improve life in other areas.

- We need to consider colonising other worlds because our population is too large for the earth and we are using up all our natural resources.
- Space exploration can encourage nations to work together.

Against
- It is expensive, especially in times of economic difficulty for many countries.
- Technological developments may be applied to making more dangerous military hardware, such as sophisticated missile systems.
- There are too many problems on the earth we should deal with first such as war, disease and malnutrition.

3 *The key points in text 1*
- Space exploration has resulted in scientific innovations that have benefited us all.
- We should go into space as a way of solving the problems of overpopulation and dwindling natural resources.

The key points in text 2
- Space exploration is still motivated by political ambitions and rivalries.
- Space exploration is a waste of money when there are so many problems to deal with on the Earth.

4 1 N
2 This is evidence to support the second point in text 1: *To make matters worse, … dwindling rapidly.*
3 This supports the first point in text 2: *We should never forget that space exploration … astronauts into space.*
4 N
5 This supports the first point in text 1: *When Armstrong set foot on the moon, … immensely beneficial … could be applied to other fields, …*
6 N
7 This supports the second point in text 2: *Space exploration is a colossal waste of money, … priorities are wrong.*
8 N

5 A The writer is disagreeing with key point 2 in the first text.
B The writer is disagreeing with key point 1 in the second text.
C The writer is supporting key point 2 in the first text.
D The writer is supporting key point 2 in the second text.

6 A Evangelists for space exploration push the idea of colonising distant worlds, and their enthusiasm is admirable.
B This is a fair point but it overlooks what has happened since.
C Despite the cost of mining such metals on the surface of neighbouring planets and asteroids, it may be the only option open to us.
D It can be argued that turning our backs on the space programme shows a lack of vision and imagination.

7 a This is too informal for an essay. It might be better in an article.
b This is a limited and unimaginative opening to an essay. The sentence structure is very basic and the vocabulary (e.g. *big*) is below the level expected from Advanced students.
c This is a good opening to an essay. The style is appropriately formal. It introduces the topic of space exploration in an interesting way, and the phrase *yet it remains highly controversial* tells the reader that the essay will probably contain an analysis of the advantages and disadvantages.
d This is not really suitable for the opening paragraph of the essay. It is dealing with a very specific point (the first one made in text 1) but doesn't work well as a general introduction to the topic of space exploration.

8 a This is not a good idea. It makes your essay rather repetitive and possibly boring. You do not have the space or time to repeat yourself if the word limit is only 280 words.
b This is the best approach to take when writing the conclusion. If you can include something new – either a new idea or argument or possibly some new facts or figures – it helps end your essay strongly and in a memorable way.
c This is possible, but it is always better to have a strong opinion in an essay, especially when you are writing no more than 280 words. An essay that is very balanced or doesn't reach a clear conclusion can be dull, and in fact may not say very much.

Optional writing task
Possible answer

Although space exploration captured the imagination of previous generations, it attracts rather less media interest today. At first sight this may be because serious problems such as global warming are so overwhelming that venturing into space feels like a distraction from more urgent issues. Landing on Mars, some people argue, will not alleviate the suffering of the millions of people struggling to get enough food to eat every day. However, if we examine the precise nature of some of the challenges the world now faces, the idea that space exploration is self-indulgent becomes hard to defend. The world's resources are finite, yet we remain committed to the dream of constant economic growth, which can only come about as a result of depleting our limited supplies of precious metals even further. All we need to power future expansion can be found on other worlds in the solar system, and that is where we should therefore turn our attention.

Cynics will say that space exploration is merely a political game, but the picture is more complex than they would have us believe. The level of international co-operation on space programmes is now considerable, and has helped reduce the possibility of future conflict between the nations involved in such projects.

In addition, it cannot be denied that scientists made a series of important technological advances when trying to get astronauts into space that have long-lasting benefits here on earth (for example the invention of pacemakers).

The way forward is clear. Nations must combine their efforts to colonise other worlds and in doing so will find practical technical solutions that will ensure the long-term survival of the human race here and in space.

(279 words)

Writing workout 4 Article

1 1 B 2 B 3 H 4 H 5 A 6 B 7 A 8 H
9 H 10 H

2 *Suggested answers*
1 A adventure   B commuting
2 B convenience   A power
3 A glamour   B reliability
4 B economy   A performance
5 B practicality   A thrills
6 B comfort   A style

3 1 combination   4 performance
2 handling   5 Features
3 capacity   6 models

Optional writing task

If possible, show your article to your teacher. Otherwise, once you have worked through exercises 4–9, compare it with the version in the Key for exercise 9.

4 **A** There is a clear angle here which relates well to the magazine feature topic. The paragraph is well constructed and quite informative, though likely to appeal more to existing riders than possible newcomers. The style and tone are neutral and appropriate for most purposes, though the paragraph is a bit bland.

B This paragraph aims to involve and intrigue the reader from the outset, using a personal approach. Again there is a clear angle which relates well to the magazine feature topic and again the paragraph is quite informative. This time, though, potential new riders may well be intrigued to read on. The style and tone are direct and informal with good use of stylistic devices – well-suited to a college magazine.

C This paragraph doesn't have a clear angle that relates to the magazine feature topic, neither does it sit well as an article opener – apparently quite complete in itself for what it is. The approach is too personal and the style rather colloquial.

5 1 just   5 To date
2 already   6 along with
3 still   7 all
4 but   8 when
The paragraph is closest in style to **B** in exercise 4.

6 **a** trips   **d** travelling
b the more usual transportation   **e** stops
c running   **f** machine

7 And (what is) the source of such a wonderful mix of convenience, economy and adventure? Well, it's a Honda, but not a Fireblade – a Foresight. Yes, 250cc of value for money and dependability, its *aerodynamic bodywork* is still state-of-the-art, with a comfortable *padded seat* and a handy *luggage compartment*. It won't pull wheelies, but it will hold a steady 120 kph and comfortably cover 700+ kilometres without refuelling.

8 All four points could apply.
Possible answer
Together we've criss-crossed Europe, we've made our way through the heat and dust of the Middle East's deserts and we've negotiated some of Africa's most spectacular bush roads. That's a lot to ask of a 4x4, let alone a two-wheeler, but the Foresight has lived up to all my hopes and stood up well to these arduous conditions. Apart from a few little dents and scratches, it still looks almost new. So, motorcycle or scooter? As far as I'm concerned, there's only one answer to that question.

9 **a** This is the catchiest of the three titles and points forward to the article in a way b and c don't. It also avoids the (potentially alienating) use of the first person I.
Full version

Travelling with Foresight …
Mention motorbikes and most people think of speed, excitement, glamour, adventure and the freedom of the open road. Mention scooters, on the other hand, and more mundane considerations like economy, comfort, convenience, practicality and reliability probably come to mind. Yet scooters make up an important part of the two-wheeled market. Are they really all bought by sad individuals who can't hack a real bike? If that's what you think, read on and prepare to be surprised.

At just over ten years old, the two-wheeler I own has already clocked up 150,000 km and is still going strong. It was purchased for travel, not for showing off or racing between motorway service areas, but for covering long distances economically, conveniently and comfortably. To date, I have covered 34 different countries on various adventure expeditions, along with using the bike for the usual convenient commuting at home – all on incredibly low fuel consumption, sustaining motorway speeds when cruising steadily along on roads.

And the source of such a wonderful mix of convenience, economy and adventure? Well, it's a Honda, but not a Fireblade – a humble Foresight. Yes, 250cc of value for money and dependability, its aerodynamic bodywork is still state-of-the-art, with a comfortable padded seat and a handy luggage compartment. It won't pull wheelies, but it will hold a steady 120 kph and comfortably cover 700+ kilometres without refuelling.

Together we've criss-crossed Europe, we've made our way through the heat and dust of the Middle East's deserts and we've negotiated some of Africa's most spectacular bush roads. That's a lot to ask of a 4x4, let alone a two-wheeler, but the Foresight has lived up to all my hopes and stood up well to these arduous conditions. Apart from a few little dents and scratches, it still looks almost new. So, motorcycle or scooter? As far as I'm concerned, there's only one answer to that question.

(316 words)

Writing workout 5 Report

1 a purpose
   b the target reader
   c content plan
   d a brief introduction
   e bullets and signposting
   f neutral tone
   g grammatical structures
   h the point
   i the target reader

2 The course is for people who need to design and produce printed material on a computer without having had any relevant training. DTP is *desktop publishing*.

Optional writing task

If possible, show your report to your teacher. Otherwise, once you have worked through exercises 3–7, compare it with the version in the Key for exercise 7.

3 The paragraph starts more like a letter (*My reason for writing* ...), the purpose of the report is unclear and personal references (*My/I/me*) are best avoided in reports. Although it can be a good idea to summarise a report's content in the introduction, this should be brief. Here *Let me begin* ... is inappropriate style for a report and the final sentence (*I'll then … recommendation.*) sounds more like an oral presentation than a written report.

Possible rewrite:
The purpose of this report is to review and assess *Good Design using DTP* with a view to determining its suitability as a course for other untrained DTP users within this organisation. The report looks first at general arrangements, before going on to course content and concluding with an evaluation.

4 *Possible answer*
The course took place at The Training Centre in Regent Street, London, on January 13–14. The facilities at the centre were excellent. The computing room was a good size, well equipped and comfortable; each participant had a dedicated computer terminal for the course duration.

The course was attended by a total of seven participants, all of whom had had some experience of – but no training in – DTP. Essentially it was a homogeneous group of beginners with compatible interests and abilities.

Arrangements throughout were faultless and timings consistently punctual. There was a good supply of refreshments during the day and considerable trouble had been taken with the lunches, which were very enjoyable.

(112 words)

5 *Corrected paragraph*
The *two*-day programme was quite intensive, covering a range of DTP functions and features, including:

- *soft*ware
- layout
- proofing
- typography
- graphics

Throughout the course was highly *practical*, with ample exercises. Comprehensive notes were provided for reference and participants were also given a copy of their completed work on disk.

6 The style and tone are too informal for a report. Colloquial expressions like *chap*, *knows a thing or two*, etc., are inappropriate, as are the contracted verb forms, the repeated use of personal pronouns, the direct question and the use of the imperative.

Possible rewrite
The tutor was Cambridge-based Will Render, a well-known expert who teaches regularly at the centre. He is obviously very knowledgeable about DTP and a skilled teacher. His approach was extremely accommodating, seeking to tailor aspects of the course to suit group and individual requirements.

The course was both enjoyable and informative, equipping participants with a sound grasp of the mechanics of DTP, and giving them the confidence to use DTP to full effect within their professional lives. Anyone using DTP without a design background would benefit enormously from this course.

7 *Possible answer*

Good Design using DTP

The purpose of this report is to review and assess *Good Design using DTP* with a view to determining its suitability as a course for other untrained DTP users within this organisation. The report looks first at general arrangements, before going on to course content and concluding with an evaluation.

General arrangements

The course took place at The Training Centre in Regent Street, London, on January 13–14. The facilities at the centre were excellent. The computing room was a good size, well equipped and comfortable; each participant had a dedicated computer terminal for the course duration.

The course was attended by a total of seven participants, all of whom had had some experience of – but no training in – DTP. Essentially it was a homogeneous group of beginners with compatible interests and abilities.

Arrangements throughout were faultless and timings consistently punctual. There was a good supply of refreshments during the day and considerable trouble had been taken with the lunches, which were very enjoyable.

Course content

The two-day programme was quite intensive, covering a range of DTP functions and features, including:

- software
- layout
- proofing
- typography
- graphics

Throughout the course was highly practical, with ample exercises. Comprehensive notes were provided for reference and participants were also given a copy of their completed work on disk.

The tutor was Cambridge-based Will Render, a well-known expert who teaches regularly at the centre. He is obviously very knowledgeable about DTP and a skilled teacher. His approach was extremely accommodating, seeking to tailor aspects of the course to suit group and individual requirements.

Evaluation and recommendation

The course was both enjoyable and informative, equipping participants with a sound grasp of the mechanics of DTP, and giving them the confidence to use DTP to full effect within their professional lives. Anyone using DTP without a design background would benefit enormously from this course.

(318 words)

Acknowledgements

The authors would like to thank the editorial team of Una Yeung, Alyson Maskell and Sarah Brierley for their help and advice in preparing this second edition, and also the coursebook authors Annette Capel and Wendy Sharp.

This product is informed by the English Vocabulary Profile, built as part of English Profile, a collaborative programme designed to enhance the learning, teaching and assessment of English worldwide. Its main funding partners are Cambridge University Press and Cambridge ESOL and its aim is to create a 'profile' for English linked to the Common European Framework of Reference for Languages (CEFR). English Profile outcomes, such as the English Vocabulary Profile, will provide detailed information about the language that learners can be expected to demonstrate at each CEFR level, offering a clear benchmark for learners' proficiency. For more information, please visit www.englishprofile.org

Development of this publication has made use of the Cambridge English Corpus (CEC). The CEC is a computerised database of contemporary spoken and written English which currently stands at over one billion words. It includes British English, American English and other varieties of English. It also includes the Cambridge Learner Corpus, developed in collaboration with the University of Cambridge ESOL Examinations. Cambridge University Press has built up the CEC to provide evidence about language use that helps to produce better language teaching materials.

The Cambridge Advanced Learner's Dictionary is the world's most widely used dictionary for learners of English. Including all the words and phrases that learners are likely to come across, it also has easy-to-understand definitions and example sentences to show how the word is used in context. The Cambridge Advanced Learner's Dictionary is available online at dictionary.cambridge.org. © Cambridge University Press, 3rd edition, 2008. Reproduced with permission.

Text acknowledgements:
The authors and publishers acknowledge the following sources of copyright material and are grateful for the permissions granted. While every effort has been made, it has not always been possible to identify the sources of all the material used, or to trace all copyright holders. If any omissions are brought to our notice, we will be happy to include the appropriate acknowledgements on reprinting.

The Times for the text on p. 5 adapted from 'Sorry Honey I shrunk your job prospects' by Morag Preston, The Times 08.04.00, for the text on p. 6 adapted from 'Barefoot doctors' by Anthony Sattin, The Times 07.01.01, for the text on p. 15 adapted from 'Concrete Jungle' by Joseph Dunn, The Sunday Times 11.05.03, for the text on pp. 28–29 adapted from 'America's first family' by Nick Griffiths, The Times 15.04.00, for the text on p. 55 adapted from 'We live in one of the wettest countries in the world' by Richard Girling, The Sunday Times Magazine 23.11.03, for the text on pp. 68–69 adapted from 'Cheer up life only gets better' by Matt Ridley, The Sunday Times 16.05.10. Copyright © The Times 2000, 2001, 2003, 2010; Guardian News and Media Ltd for the text on p. 9 (text 3) adapted from 'Weather outlook 5-day forecast', The Observer 25.06.00, for the text on p. 11 (ex 9) adapted from 'Two for the Road' by Jim Whyte, The Guardian 22.11.03, for the text on p. 20 adapted from 'Ethical shopping' by George Monbiot, The Guardian 24.07.07, for the text on p. 23 adapted from 'One woman in five is a shopaholic' by Tracey McVeigh, The Observer 26.11.00, for the text on p. 44 adapted from 'Fighting talk' by Dolly Dhingra, The Guardian 30.10.00, for the text on p. 51 adapted from 'Mind your peas' by Robin McKie, The Observer 18.06.00, for the text on pp. 52–53 adapted from 'Blooms with a view' by Mike Herd, The Guardian 25.06.11, for the text on p. 57 (ex 3) adapted from 'The Intelligent consumer' by Jane Clarke, The Observer 09.07.00, for the text on p. 59 adapted from 'Fat boy is workout king' by Denis Campbell, The Observer 11.02.01, for the text on p. 75 adapted from 'Good vibrations' by Wendy Moore, The Observer 11.02.01, for the text on pp. 76–77 adapted from 'I'm being honest about my dishonesty' by Decca Aitkenhead, The Guardian 18.10.10, for the text on pp. 86–87 (ex 2B and 3) adapted from 'Pintermime time' by Susannah Clapp, The Observer 09.12.01. Copyright Guardian News & Media Ltd 2000, 2003, 2007, 2011, 2001, 2010; New Scientist for the text on p. 9 (text 2) adapted from 'Astrium Recruitment Advertisement', New Scientist Magazine 24.06.00, for the text on pp. 12–13 adapted from 'It's not fair! Gimme that food!' by Frans de Waal, New Scientist Magazine 14.11.09. Reproduced with permission; Wexas Ltd for the text on p. 11 (ex 8) adapted from 'Fear of flying' by Sheila Critchley, Traveller's Handbook, published by Wexas 1998.

Reproduced with permission; The Random House Group for the text on p. 17 adapted from Madhur Jaffrey's Indian Cooking by Madhur Jaffrey, published by BBC Books. Reprinted by permission of the Random House Group Limited; The Sunday Post for the text on p. 26 adapted from 'Sex and plugs and rock 'n' roll' by Iain Harrison, The Sunday Post 06.04.08, for the text on p. 71 adapted from 'Teenager's long-forgotten memoirs make it into print' by Gary Moug, The Sunday Post 19.03.06. Reproduced with permission; The Random House Group and PFD for the text on p. 32 adapted from The Hutchinson History of the World by John Roberts, published by Hutchinson. Reprinted by permission of The Random House Group Limited and from The Pelican History of the World by J M Roberts (Copyright © J.M. Roberts 1976) by permission of PFD on behalf of Dr John Roberts; The Economist for the text on p. 35 adapted from 'Tolled you so', The Economist 22.06.00. Reproduced with permission; Ariane Batterberry for the abridged text on pp. 36–37 from Fashion: The Mirror of History by Michael Batterberry and Ariane Batterberry, introduction by Stella Blum, published by Columbus Books 1977. Reproduced with permission; The Independent for the text on p. 42 adapted from 'Globalisation should be a positive force for all' by Kofi Annan, The Independent 12.12.00, for the text on p. 43 adapted from 'Concerted action for a global problem' by Masood Ahmed, The Independent 12.12.00. Copyright © The Independent 2000; The Scotsman for the text on p. 47 adapted from 'How could I stand in the way of his dream?' by Anna Smyth, The Scotsman 31.03.05. Reproduced with permission; HarperCollins Publishers Ltd for the text on pp. 60–61 adapted from Why men don't iron, copyright © Anne Moir 1999. Reprinted by permission of HarperCollins Publishers Ltd, for the text on p. 74 adapted from Freedom at midnight, copyright © Larry Collins and Dominique Lapierre 1975. Reprinted by permission of HarperCollins Publishers Ltd; Saga Magazine for the text on p. 63 adapted from 'Going it alone' by Beth Ivory, Saga Magazine December 2001. Reproduced with permission; Daily Mail for the listening activity on p. 80 adapted from 'Revealed after 50 years: the secret of the greatest-ever student prank' by Laura Clark, Daily Mail 27.06.08. Copyright © Daily Mail; National Geographic for the text on pp. 84–85 adapted from 'Animals at play' by Stuart L Brown, National Geographic December 1994. Reproduced with permission; Oxford University Press for the text on p. 86 (ex 2A) adapted from pp. 766–767 (250 words) Oxford Companion to English Literature edited by Margaret Drabble, copyright © 1985. By permission of Oxford University Press; Telegraph Media Group Limited for the text on pp. 86–87 (ex 2B and 4) adapted from 'Echoes of what might have been' by John Gross, The Sunday Telegraph 09.12.01. Copyright © Telegraph Media Group Limited 2001; Honda EU for the text on pp. 117–118 adapted from Honda Motorcycles 2000. Reproduced with permission of Honda EU; The Publishing Training Centre for the text on pp. 118–119 adapted from 'A guide to courses and in-company training', 1998. Reproduced with permission of The Publishing Training Centre.

Photo acknowledgements:
p.8: Alamy/Kevpix; p.12: FLPA/Pete Oxford/Minden Pictures; p.15: Getty Images/Matthew Tabaccos/Barcroft Medi; p.16: Superstock/Tips Images; p.18: Getty Images/Image Source; p.23: Alamy/Paul Springett A; p.24: Getty Images/Tom Kelley Archive/Retrofile RF; p.28: Press Association Images/Chris Pizzello/AP; p.31: Rex Features/Sipa Press; p.33: Rex Features/Alisdair Macdonald; p.35: Alamy/Tom Uhlman; p.36: Alamy/Jackie Ellis; p.39: Thinkstock/Stockbyte; p.53: Robert Harding Picture Library/Heeb Christian/age footstock; p.56L: Alamy/Horizon International Images Limited; p.56C: Thinkstock/Stockbyte; p.56R: Thinkstock/istockphoto; p.59: www.GutCheckFitness.com/Joe Decker; p.60: NI Syndication/The Times; p.63: Alamy/Alistair Laming; p.68: Glowimages.com/Eye Ubiquitous; p.74: Getty Images/Keystone; p.76: Corbis/Rune Hellestad; p.78: Corbis/Frithjof Hirdes; p.84: Getty Images/Norbert Rosing/National Geographic; p.86: Photostage/Donald Cooper; p.90: Honda(UK); p.92: Alamy/Mike Booth.

Illustrator acknowledgements:
Jo Blake (Beehive Illustration) p 54; Mary Claire Smith p 66; Mark Draisey pp 4, 26, 44, 80; Nick Duffy p 70; Dylan Gibson p 58; Joanna Kerr (Meiklejohn Illustration) p 38; Julian Mosedale pp 6, 49, 64, 73; Dave Russell p 9; Rory Walker pp 43, 81

Recordings by Leon Chambers at the Soundhouse Ltd.

Picture research by Louise Edgeworth.